TOP TO TOE

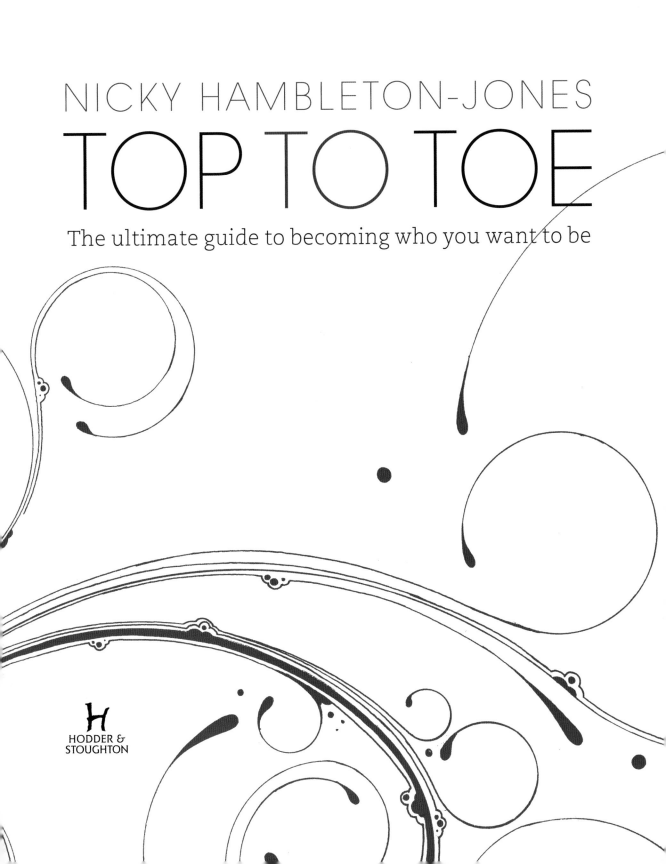

NICKY HAMBLETON-JONES
TOP TO TOE

The ultimate guide to becoming who you want to be

HODDER &
STOUGHTON

TO SUZY – WITHOUT WHOM NONE OF THIS
WOULD HAVE BEEN POSSIBLE.

First published in Great Britain in 2008 by Hodder & Stoughton

An Hachette Livre UK company

1

Copyright © Nicky Hambleton-Jones 2008
Illustrations © Si Scott 2008
Photography © Liam Duke 2008
Additional photographic sources: Alamy, Corbis, Getty Images.

A CIP catalogue record for this title is available from the British Library

ISBN 978 0 340 92413 6

Designed and typeset in Caecilia and Avant Garde Gothic by Smith & Gilmour, London

Printed and bound by Butler & Tanner, Frome, Somerset

Hodder & Stoughton policy is to use papers that are natural, renewable and recyclable
products and made from wood grown in sustainable forests. The logging and
manufacturing processes are expected to conform to the environmental regulations
of the country of origin.

Hodder & Stoughton Ltd
338 Euston Road
London NW1 3BH

www.hodder.co.uk

CONTENTS

CHAPTER ONE

Dream on

'THERE ARE SOME PEOPLE WHO LIVE IN A DREAM WORLD AND THERE ARE SOME WHO FACE REALITY; AND THEN THERE ARE THOSE WHO TURN ONE INTO THE OTHER.' DOUGLAS H. EVERETT

I was made redundant three times in the space of two years. Not a great situation to be in and I have to confess it did start to get a little embarrassing when friends phoned to say, 'Not again?'

After the first two redundancies I felt mortified and such a failure. But when it happened for the third time in February 2001, my whole perception changed. Instead of feeling humiliated I'd answer, 'Well, I'm obviously being groomed for greatness, my coping skills are as slick as they're going to get – so there must be a big plan for me out there!' That would make my friends laugh and call me crazy, but I knew deep down they admired my courage to survive. It doesn't mean I never shed any tears along the way; there were a lot of those. But I'll go into more detail about that later.

I think the worst thing about redundancy is the way you're treated like a leper as soon as the deed is done. Everyone starts awkwardly jumping around as if you're contagious. I was frogmarched into IT where the IT guy cleared everything from my PC and muttered words of condolence to me. On parting, I turned back to him and said, 'Watch this space – I'll be famous one day!' To which he replied, 'I've no doubt you will.' That was just before I was escorted out of building into the world outside.

Famous? Who was I fooling? I was two weeks away from my thirtieth birthday with a CV that resembled an unfinished patchwork quilt; I had no job, no man and a mortgage. Any sane person would tell you I didn't have a hope of being anything more than desperate. But, somewhere deep inside me, even though there wasn't any evidence to support it, I believed that I was special, that I was different and destined for greatness (whatever shape or form that took). I also knew I didn't want to live a life of predictability and monotony that would end and be forgotten as if it had never begun.

My first port of call was Paradise Cove in Mauritius. It was the middle of February and I certainly didn't want to endure another Valentine's Day single and unemployed. I packed my bags and two days after being made redundant I was on a plane heading south. A little sunshine was just what I needed to cheer up my spirits and give me time to think, I decided. Who would have thought that Paradise Cove would appeal to so many loved-up honeymooners?

Despite the happy couples, that holiday was a defining moment in my life. I spent my days lazing on the beach dreaming of the life I wanted to create – and writing. I wrote descriptions of my ideal job, my ideal lifestyle, my ideal man. At the time they were nothing more than pipe dreams, but it helped me focus on the things I really wanted. Throughout this book I will share some of those descriptions with you and I should add that I am still marvelling at how,

in less than five years, most of those dreams became reality.

One thing was for sure, three redundancies had to be a sign that I was as sure as hell never going back to the corporate world. I had to make it on my own; the question was how?

By October 2001 I was down to my last £100. I had an overdraft limit of £1,000 so at least I knew I could cover one month's mortgage payment – but then what? The euphoric feeling of freedom and purpose at the idea of being self-employed was slowly starting to seep away as reality ever so slowly tightened its grip. (I was trying to set up my personal stylist business, Tramp2Vamp at the time.)

LIVING THE DREAM

'DREAM AS IF YOU'LL LIVE FOR EVER, LIVE AS IF YOU'LL DIE TODAY.' **JAMES DEAN**

Thinking back to that time of my life still sends shivers down my spine. I'll be honest, it's not somewhere I'd like to visit again, but then I wouldn't have half the satisfaction and appreciation for every living moment of my life now if I hadn't experienced the other side.

Making the decision to change my career was the best thing I've ever done. But like any other journey you embark on, with the good also comes the bad – the tough, trying, nail-biting times when all you want to do is jump ship and get back to dry land. It was in those times that I asked myself: 'What's the worst that can happen? It doesn't work out and you get another job.' There are no guarantees with anything. Some people succeed, others don't. The point is, it's not the outcome that's important. The journey of self-discovery is worth far more than the destination. But one thing I can guarantee is that, if you continue to persevere, you will get there. It might not be exactly what you first set out to achieve, but if you tap into the lessons you will learn along the way, success will find you before you find it.

THE SKY'S THE LIMIT

At first I had the idea that I wanted global domination; I wanted to be the next Richard Branson (the female version). Everyone laughed; men ran a mile. The façade of a blonde, attractive female seemed to be masking a hidden madwoman.

Undeterred, I persevered: I wanted to create a global brand that was transferable to any number of products from make-up to clothes. I quickly realised that local domination would be a feat in itself considering I had no money and the only employee was myself, but there's no harm in aiming for the sky.

Five years on, and global domination is the furthest thing from my mind, but back then it gave me the inspiration and the energy I needed to keep going. You've got to aim high in the hope you'll get somewhere in between. What that is may be what you set out to achieve or it may be totally different. One thing is for sure, it will never be worse – it will only get better.

ANYONE CAN DO IT

In my mind all you need to change your life is belief and determination. Belief in yourself and your dream, and the determination to get out of bed every day no matter how tough it gets, or how low you feel. Never, ever give up.

This may sound easy but it takes a lot of grit and determination. Ask yourself: do you believe you're worth something better? While the answer is no, maybe, not sure, then you'll never change: you simply don't want it badly enough. That's why it's so important to really focus on that self-belief – it's the thing that will keep you going. And that's what I'm here to help you do.

'EVERY ACHIEVER I HAVE EVER MET SAYS, "MY LIFE TURNED AROUND WHEN I BEGAN TO BELIEVE IN ME."' **ROBERT SCHULLER**

Determination for change rises up like a fiery volcano from the pit of your stomach. It's the fuel that keeps you firing every day. It's the energy that gets you out of bed in the morning. It's the knowledge that you're special; that you have what it takes to be different – and you already are.

The
game plan

CHAPTER TWO

MY MISSION FOR YOU

Changing your life, whether it's your job or the way you look, can be one of the most rewarding, exhilarating experiences you'll ever have. But let's face it, the prospect of change can also be terrifying. So scary, in fact, that many choose to ignore those feelings that life really could be better than this. Sometimes we just need a little push to take the plunge.

I want this book to be your catalyst, the spark that ignites the fire within your soul. I want you to feel breathless with excitement at the prospect of change, a new beginning, a fresh start. Whether it's simply changing the way you look or totally changing what you do.

You have to feel excited, you have to feel passionate, you have to feel energised. You are about to embark on the rollercoaster ride of your life, full of extreme highs and terrifying lows; but your passion, determination and belief will remain with you and get you through no matter what.

Are you ready?

'YOU ARE NEVER TOO OLD TO SET ANOTHER GOAL OR TO DREAM A NEW DREAM.' C.S. LEWIS

I firmly believe we are all passionate about something, but most of us never ask ourselves the question what. It should be instinctive, like meeting an attractive member of the opposite sex – you know instantly whether you're attracted to them or not. In the same way, you should know instinctively what you're passionate about. I'm not suggesting this will give you that light-bulb moment, but simply acknowledging the things that you're passionate about will enable you to start structuring your life around those things you love to do.

Holiday over. It was time to decide what to do with my life. Based on the success of my previous career choices to date, I knew I needed some expert input. I remember watching Tim Henman play at Wimbledon that summer of 2001 and being so inspired by the way he'd totally transformed his game and made a comeback. The reason? He'd hired Pete Sampras's coach. I figured if anyone wanted to get to the top, they needed a top-class support team. Mine consisted of a lot of friends and the life coach, Suzy Greaves.

I'll never forget my first coaching call with Suzy. The first thing she asked me was, 'What are you passionate about?' To which I replied, 'Fashion!' I remember being so taken aback by my reply that I looked around the room to see if someone else was there. I had qualifications in clinical nutrition, statistics, finance and marketing, with work experience in IT and management consulting – nothing at all to do with fashion. What was I talking about?

A PASSION FOR ...

You see, right from an early age I'd had a love of fashion and clothes, but I never pursued it – I thought it was fanciful and not suitable as a long-term career. So I buried this passion deeper and deeper until I'd almost forgotten about it.

After three redundancies, my career was in such a state that I was too scared to allow myself to consider starting something new for fear of another disappointment. It's easy to fail at things you're not that passionate about, but what if you follow your passion in order to fulfil your dreams and still fail? What do you have left?

What I didn't realise was that, when you follow your passion, life becomes easier. By this I don't mean that all your problems disappear, but at least you feel as though you're swimming with the tide instead of straining against it. When I worked in the City, everything seemed a struggle.

One of the reasons I think I never really cracked it in the City was because – quite frankly – I didn't give a toss what company merged with what company, what new IT system needed to be installed, and which procedures needed to be written. Reading the *Financial Times* was a sweat; browsing the fashion pages of *Vogue*, on the other hand, was pure pleasure and unadulterated fun. No matter how hard I tried to feign interest, I just couldn't quite muster up the enthusiasm required to excel in the job … and it showed. I constantly felt like I had toffee stuck to the bottom of my shoes. Everything was an effort, nothing came easily, and yet I continued to struggle through miserably, hoping that one day something would change.

And change it did, but it still took three redundancies to make me wake up and realise just maybe the City wasn't for me.

As the saying goes, until you learn the lesson you never leave the classroom. If the same thing keeps going wrong over and over again, stop blaming the world and think about the lesson. It's the quickest way to put it behind you and move on.

Which brings me back to passion. When you do something you love, opportunities arise where you least expect them. I'm not saying you don't have to work hard to find them, but it no longer feels like pulling teeth.

STRATEGY FOR SUCCESS

The road to success is different for everyone. There are no rules: what works for one person may not work for another. The important thing is that you find your own way, one that works for you.

I devised a strategy for success that works for me which can be applied to any aspect of life that you want to change. I'm not suggesting it's fail proof, but it should give you the inspiration you need to keep going.

'WHAT IS NOT STARTED TODAY IS NEVER FINISHED TOMORROW.' **GOETHE**

Whether you're embarking on a new career or simply reinventing the way you look, the first step towards success is to have a dream or vision. It may be a dream about what you want to do, how you want to live, who you'd like to marry, or simply how you'd like to look. No matter how big or how small, it's extremely hard to change without a vision. Some may refer to this as a goal, but for me the difference between a dream and a goal is emotion. Our lives are constantly bogged down with goals: some we achieve – some we don't. Either way we operate our lives according to what we need to do or aim for next. Where's the excitement? Where's the passion? Where's the dream?

GOALS, DREAMS AND INTENTIONS

Goals make dreams happen. It can help to think of them as the doing, the list of things you tick off, but without a dream a list of goals becomes nothing more than a chore. *Dreams* apply to every aspect of your life – what you do, how you feel about yourself, or how you would like to look.

For example, if your dream is to own a pair of Jimmy Choos, your goal is to save up enough money to afford them. Perhaps your dream is to climb Mount Kilimanjaro. Your goals will be incorporated into a rigorous training programme that will ensure you become fit enough to be able to reach the top and achieve your dream.

The big difference between a goal and a dream is in the emotion. Achieving your goals makes you feel good about yourself and in control of your destiny. Achieving your dreams is totally exhilarating and makes you want to scream, laugh or cry – it's a release of pent-up emotion. Goals are the building blocks that drive you towards achieving your dream.

From the moment we start school our lives become defined by a series of goals, but very few dreams. I believe the more we can define ourselves by our dreams the more fulfilled and happy we will be.

'THE ONLY THING THAT WILL STOP YOU FULFILLING YOUR DREAMS IS YOU.' **TOM BRADLEY**

There's no limit to the number of dreams you can have, and when you've achieved one – it's time for the next.

A few of my dreams

★ I've always wanted to learn another language – Spanish and Italian are my favourites.

★ I'd love to be able to achieve a black belt in a martial art (not sure what yet but that comes later – this is only about our dreams).

★ I'd love to own a villa in Italy or a house in Dorset – so perhaps learning Italian might be more useful.

★ I'd love to learn how to cook really well, but this is probably at the bottom of my list at the moment.

★ Oh, and I've always wanted to be able to play tennis properly. I seriously lack eye-ball coordination, so that could be a bit of a challenge, but dreams and reality don't have to mix.

Dreams can be big or small; the important thing is to have them. Dreams give us a reason to live and love life. They are what make the goals worth achieving.

Most of us are too scared to dream in case it emphasises the banality of our existence. Perhaps a dream is so far removed from our reality that it seems a frivolous luxury even to attempt to think about what could have been. But the truth is, it still can happen. I want you to leave your comfort zone and just consider for one moment…what if?

If the security guard who frogmarched me from the building had turned around to me and said, 'Hey don't worry, you'll have your own primetime TV series in two years' time,' I think I would have thought he'd lost his mind.

ANYTHING CAN HAPPEN

Who is to say what you can or can't do or achieve? People love giving you their opinion, but in actual fact you are the master of your own destiny. You – and only you – can make things happen. I know it sounds daunting and sometimes all we want is for someone to come along and swish their magic wand to make things happen, but it wouldn't be any fun or half as rewarding if you didn't have to work for it, now would it? If it were easy, everyone would do it.

'THINK HIGHLY OF YOURSELF BECAUSE THE WORLD TAKES YOU AT YOUR OWN ESTIMATE.' **ANON**

Dreams are what you make of them. They keep the blood pumping in our veins; they're our reason to live. You are never too old or too young to dream. Your dreams are highly personal and something that no one can ever take away from you. Whatever your situation – dare to dream.

BE YOURSELF

My big dreams centred on career and lifestyle. Not so much a specific job, but more the type of environment I needed to be in to enable me to perform at my best – and, most importantly, to be me. If there's one thing in life we all excel at, it's being ourselves. No one will ever master it quite like you do, so the most important thing when developing your dream is to do something where you can just be you.

Mauritius, February 2001 – Nicky's dream lifestyle

Lying on a beach in Mauritius two weeks after being made redundant, I listed everything that would make up my dream lifestyle, in no particular order:

★ I would like to earn enough money to invest in a number of properties.

★ I see my main home being in the country where I'm able to have friends and family to stay and entertain endlessly.

★ I would like to have a number of staff to support me in running the household, including a cook, cleaner, nanny, gardener and possibly a driver too. (Not asking too much then?)

★ I would like to be able to go away to the Caribbean or some exotic island at least once a year.

★ I would like to have a tennis court on my property where I can play tennis with my husband (who I haven't yet met, but that's a minor detail – see 'Dream Man' spec on page 194) on a summer's evening.

★ I would like to keep a flat in London, which a member of my family could rent out or where we can stay if working in London.

★ I would love to own a sports car just once in my life for fun.

★ I want a home that is hospitable, where friends can stay for the weekend and relax.

★ I want to feel that I've achieved in every aspect of my life – home, work and play … not an easy task, perhaps too ambitious?

★ I would like to be in a position where I am wealthy in my own right and never have to worry about earning money again (considering I have less than £10K to my name right now, or £8.5K once I've paid for the holiday, I'm only asking for a minor miracle).

It was a pipe dream at the time, one that was so far removed from my reality that even I found it amusing, but the great thing is that we're all entitled to dream – no matter how bizarre or far fetched our dreams might be. It's our dreams that help us escape from reality and keep us going when we need reminding why it is we're doing what we do. So now you know about my dream life, what's yours?

DARE TO DREAM

Before you read on, I want you to take an hour out of your daily routine. Go somewhere away from everything and everyone. The park, an art gallery, take a boat on the river, a walk on the beach, or catch a train – just go somewhere you can clear your mind of all its clutter and set it free to dream of a life you'd like to create, or things you want to achieve. The pace of life makes it very difficult to take time out of the routines that govern us and dare to imagine something different. This is your opportunity, so go for it.

A QUESTION OF INTENT

By now you've hopefully resurrected your dreams. The next challenge is converting them into reality, and by this I mean building a visual picture of what your dreams will look like. These are what I call intentions.

Intentions are closely aligned with your dreams but they're more specific. They're almost like a description of your dream. Let's go back to the Jimmy Choo example.

Your dream is to own a pair of Jimmy's. Your intentions would look something like this:

★ I want to buy my first pair of Jimmy's by March 2009
★ They will be pillar-box red, made from leather
★ They'll have a peep toe and a long thin stiletto heel in metallic gold

Or take your dream of climbing Mount Kilimanjaro.
Your intentions are:
★ To complete the climb by June 2009
★ To reach the summit in four days (not sure if that's realistic
or not, but you get the picture)
★ To be at peak fitness before you start

The reason intentions are so important is because they help you
visualise what your dream will look like – the specifics. By detailing
out the elements and intricacies of your dream you will start to
visualise it. The clearer the picture you build in your mind, the
greater your chance of achieving it.

Trust me, this works! I've proved it to myself time and time again.
A couple of years ago Rob, my gorgeous husband (whom I met in
2003) and I wanted to buy a house. We sat down and wrote out a list
describing every detail of our dream home. The whole point about
a wish list is to be as specific as you like. It's for your eyes only and
it really helps give you clarity about what you do really want and
more importantly about what you don't.

After writing the wish list for our dream home, I stashed it in
a handbag that I rarely use and only discovered it again after we'd
actually moved into our new home a year later. As I read through my
wish list I felt the hairs on my neck stand on end. I could tick almost
every detail on my list – my dream home had become a reality.

CLEAR INTENTIONS

It never ceases to amaze me how powerful setting out your intentions
can be. One of the main reasons I think it works is because it gives
you clarity. When we were registering with estate agents, we were
able to be very specific about what we were looking for. Anything that
didn't meet our criteria we didn't waste our time on.

We must have registered with about ten estate agents, but it was only when we sat down with the last one and reeled off our criteria that she pulled out a property spec saying, 'I think this may be what you're looking for.' As soon as I saw the floor plan and the location, I knew this was it. It was the only appointment we made and the only property we viewed. The whole process was effortless and fun.

If your intentions are really clear, you are less likely to waste time on a tangent when it doesn't comply with your wish list. Focus is critical when pursuing a dream. You will be significantly challenged along the way, and to survive you need to be really clear about what it is you are aiming for, otherwise you will easily be led astray.

YOUR GOALS

Our lives are constantly defined by goals; it is important that you don't confuse your goals with your dreams or intentions.

★ The dream is the big picture
★ The intention is the detail
★ The goal is the to-do list

The big difference between your intentions and your goals is that there should be no sense of guilt if you don't achieve everything you *intend* to. Intentions are much more a gentle, sure, all-pervading knowledge of what it is you want and what you are aspiring to.

If you ever get confused, just trust your gut instinct. If something feels like an effort and doesn't get you excited, it's probably a goal. If you're beating yourself up because you haven't done what you wanted to do – it's definitely a goal.

So next time you allow yourself to dream, don't just think it, put pen to paper and describe it in detail, then watch this space.

HOW HUNGRY ARE YOU?

It's not enough to think, 'Wouldn't it be nice if …?' or 'Maybe one day I'd like to …'. Your need for change has to burn a hole through your soul. It has to make you itch like you're covered in eczema – you have to want it so badly that the idea of life continuing the way it is seems worse than death. I know I'm being a little melodramatic but you get the idea – you have to be desperate. If you're not desperate for change, you'll very easily cave in and run for cover at the first hurdle. And this applies to every aspect of your life, whether you're trying to lose weight, change your style, your job or your whole life. We are all constrained by our comfort zones. These are the limiting factors in our lives, the things that prevent us from crossing over to the other side and achieving success.

When you're 'desperate', you're more likely to take risks. The nature of risk means hurling yourself into uncharted territory, not knowing the outcome but trusting that it will be better than where you are now. You have to be prepared to challenge the boundaries of the zones of comfort that we all establish in our lives to protect us from fear. The only thing that will give you the confidence to expose yourself to the elements is hunger: hunger for self-discovery, hunger for change, hunger for success or just a different way of life.

FEELING THE PINCH

When I got down to my last £100, it was almost as if life went into slow motion; the calm before the storm. At first I felt quite matter of fact about it, almost not quite believing the situation I was in. Slowly but surely, the reality started to take hold and all I wanted to do was run for cover. I was petrified. There is possibly nothing more suffocating than not having any money. You simply can't do anything, and the less you try to do the more you're confronted with your lack of it.

So there I was, clinging on for dear life to the edge of comfort, desperate to pull myself back and crawl into safety. But then I realised that there is no such thing as safety. Had I not been desperate for a better life, desperate not to have to go crawling back to the City in pieces begging for a job, I would have fallen back into my zone and for the rest of my life I would have asked myself, 'What if?'

I used to wonder, if you want something badly enough, how far would you go to get it? What's your limit? I truly believe if you're hungry enough you will never be pushed past your limit of control. No matter how bad it gets, it will always be within your power to deal with.

After I'd finally confronted the dire financial situation I was in, I realised that not only did I not want to give up, but that I had to find a way to survive. I decided to rent out my flat and move in with friends. For a year I moved between friends every couple of weeks. I was like a nomad. I practically lived out of my car.

Looking back on that year now, I just don't know how I did it – or how my friends did it! But the point is I did, and at the end of it I was able to go back into rented accommodation. It enabled me to maintain the cash flow to sustain my business. I really believe it was my hunger for success that gave me the determination to survive, whatever it took – that and the support and hospitality of my friends.

TIMETABLE FOR CHANGE

I remember countless occasions when I became so frustrated by the sloth-like pace at which I seemed to be progressing. There is no point more disheartening than when the initial euphoria of the prospect of change has worn off and reality hits – whether you're changing a career or embarking on a new physique. It takes time, some more time and then some … and just when you thought you were turning the corner – you don't.

Looking back on the five years since I left my City job and started my own business, a lot has happened and my life has changed dramatically. To some it might seem very fast, but I can assure you to me it felt like a lifetime. The only thing that got me through those dark times when I seemed to have been treading water for an eternity was my commitment to following my dream.

One of the most frustrating things about change is that no one can tell you how long it will take or how things will turn out. This is an entry in my diary that illustrates my attitude to time.

Monday 24 May 2004

Another dire day in my 'office', I feel demotivated, bored and I am going crazy working on my own all day. I look at my calendar for the week ahead and, bar a meeting tomorrow afternoon, I have nada on. Nothing! How does that happen? You work your butt off for six months and yet nothing's changed. Everyone keeps telling me to be patient. What? I've been slogging away for three years but so far nothing has really changed.

I feel really miserable and just want to curl up into a ball and die. Why does life have to be so hard? I thought things were supposed to happen effortlessly?

Maybe tomorrow will be better?!

I know, I'm all about drama! They say the first five years of starting your own business are the worst and I can categorically confirm that's true. Obviously how long it takes will depend upon what or how much of your life you're trying to change, but I was going for the whole package. I wanted it all, and I wanted it *now*.

TIME CHALLENGE

For me, time was one of my biggest challenges – it's the void of nothingness when everything seems to grind to a halt; the times when nothing's going right and the only direction you seem to move is backwards. There is no light at the end of the tunnel, you don't even know if you're in the right tunnel – but you've simply got to keep going.

Just to make it harder, your 'Get Out of Jail' card will be dangled in front of you constantly, goading and tantalising you. Even your friends start questioning your decisions. You will certainly start considering other options and questioning the choices you've made. This is when all your dreams and beliefs are pushed to the limit.

If you don't strongly believe in what you're doing, time will eat you alive.

The same principle applies to every aspect of life, from changing careers, relationships, losing weight or embarking on an exercise regime. It takes time before you really start to see results, which is why most people give up and never break the cycle. Change doesn't happen overnight; you need to give it time.

YOUR DREAM TEAM

So far it's all been about you – your dreams, your passion, your intentions and beliefs. Now it's time to think about the role other people play. By this I mean building a network of people around you who can guide and support you while you follow your dream; the people who really believe in you and all you are trying to achieve. Don't forget, whatever you're trying to change, you are embarking on a journey, a little like a rollercoaster ride where the highs are thrilling and the lows make you want to give up and go home.

I honestly believe that had it not been for my friends there is no way I would have survived. I would have given up long before I came close to achieving anything. At my lowest, darkest moments, when even I stopped believing in myself, my friends would step in, pick me up off the ground, take me out for dinner and make me laugh. It broke the fall. I no longer felt I was plummeting into the pit of gloom. All of a sudden, life wouldn't seem so bad. It gave me the confidence to pick up the pieces and carry on. More importantly, they never stopped believing in me, long after I'd stopped believing in myself.

Following your dream can be all consuming and emotionally draining at times. Maintaining a sense of normality and fun is important if the journey is going to be a memorable one.

Choosing your team

When choosing your support team, be very selective.

★ Make sure you only surround yourself with people you can trust and who really believe in what you're doing.

★ Your partner can be your best and most loyal supporter, but it's up to you to keep him involved so he knows what's going on and doesn't feel left behind. After all, he's going on this exciting ride with you. Although I only met my husband Rob a few years into setting up my business and going it alone, he still maintains I wouldn't have achieved half of it without him, and I think that's true. He gives me the freedom to fly, and I know that he'll catch me if I fall.

★ You need friends who will keep you on the straight and narrow when you want to jump ship and go back to your old ways.

★ Think about your friends as the safety harness on the rollercoaster holding and supporting you. If one of them has any doubts, they will waver and you'll come crashing down. You simply can't afford it.

★ You need to surround yourself with champions: people who truly believe in you and your dream.

★ You also need people who will offer practical help – extra childcare for instance – or support and advice when those closest to you feel threatened by change.

'A FRIEND IS SOMEONE WHO LETS YOU HAVE TOTAL FREEDOM TO BE YOURSELF.' JIM MORRISON

At various points along the way you will also need to call on specialists – people who will share their expertise and guide you in the right direction. I can't stress enough just how important it is to only surround yourself with people who really believe in you.

For example, if you're trying to lose weight you need a personal trainer who really believes you will achieve your goals, not someone who's simply doing a job. If you're looking for a bank loan, you want a bank manager who is inspired by what you're trying to do and will give you the informed advice you need.

Sometimes, belief and connection are more important than credentials. Your champions will move heaven and earth to make sure you stay on the straight and narrow. Whether they're the best in their field is irrelevant – you need people who understand and 'get' you.

Along the way I had many life coaches, all of whom were very good at what they did, but only one remained my cornerstone throughout – because she 'got' me. Suzy knew exactly what to say when I was feeling despondent. She knew what inspired me, what excited me and what made me tick. So many others simply didn't press the buttons I needed to get out of bed in the morning and carry on.

I can't stress enough how important it is to make sure the chemistry's right when you're choosing people for your A-team. You need to be confident that they'll be there when the going gets tough, that they see the hidden potential within you, and that they'll keep on believing in you long after your first cry for help.

DEMONS AND FEARS

I have to confess, I'm not an adrenaline junkie. I don't like heights or speed, so anything remotely dangerous that could result in an injury of any kind is simply not for me. I find it utterly paralysing and I'm literally unable to put one foot in front of the other. Yet, when it comes to taking financial, emotional or career risks it's a different story – or at least that's what I thought.

In the beginning, when I'd decided to start Tramp2Vamp (my personal styling business), I spent weeks writing a business plan and formulating all sorts of ideas in my head. I even held a brainstorming session with friends and asked them for their input and suggestions. I spent hours devising all sorts of world domination strategies that looked very impressive on paper, but in reality amounted to nothing.

Then out of the blue (or so it seemed), Suzy said to me, 'It's time you started making some money and put that business plan to use. It's time you got yourself some clients.'

It was as if she'd thrown icy water over me. What? Actually go out there and do something? But I've never done this before. What if I'm hopeless at it? What if I fail? I felt sick. So I handled it in my usual 'style', which is denial. I spent the afternoon with friends and continued to dream. That felt better, except deep down of course it didn't.

I'll never forget walking back into my flat to the phone ringing. I picked it up, wondering if it was my next blind date calling to confirm dinner for tomorrow evening. Nothing like knowing your priorities.

But instead I heard a female voice saying, 'My name's Rachel, I heard you were a personal stylist, and I was just wondering if I could book a session with you?'

'Um ... sure, when were you thinking of?' I replied. (All the while hoping she would answer, 'In a month's time,' which would keep Suzy off my back for longer.)

'Tomorrow?'

What?! 'Yip, no problem,' I said and took down her details.

As soon as I hung up I started doing hopscotch around the flat in the hope that it might solve the problem of what to do. It didn't and I ended up stubbing my toe on the table. To cut a long story short, I did it. And, not only that, I did a brilliant job – which was the turning point for me and totally life-changing for Rachel, who has looked like a diva ever since. Throwing myself into the deep end, with the help of vixens Suzy and Rachel, was the best thing that ever happened to me. Sometimes in life, no matter how good our intentions, we simply need a push.

FEAR LESS

There is a practical and emotional side to fear. Whilst working in the corporate world, I was constantly in fear of losing my job. I was in fear of the implications this would have on my life – how would I survive? How would I afford to shop? How would I pay the mortgage? Holidays? My fear was that life would be miserable.

Fears are different for everyone. For some of you they centre on the people you support and are responsible for – children who depend on your time and your income. Partners can also be resistant to change, feeling comfortable with the person they know. Perhaps your worry is that they won't like the new you and might even leave.

Whatever your private fears, the key thing I didn't realise at the time was that life was more miserable living in fear of losing my job than actually losing it (although I admit it did take me three redundancies to realise this – but then I am a blonde at heart, after all).

My point is that when your worst fears actually come true and you think life will start to tumble all around you, it's never as bad as you think. You will always come up with a plan. Just trust in yourself and those around you. Often the things we fear most are not as terrible as we imagine and can even improve the relationships we already have.

When embarking on a change project, we need all the love and support we can get. But at the end of the day the only person you can really rely on and trust in life is *you*. Don't get me wrong, I'm not suggesting you shouldn't trust anyone – I've already stressed the importance of friendly support. I'm just trying to make you believe in your own power, the internal strength that you haven't even tapped into yet. It's all very well getting your friends and family on board, but only you can make things happen; only you can fulfil your dreams. If you trust yourself enough then you'll no longer be controlled by fear. You will be able to move forward knowing that, whatever happens, you'll find a solution.

Fear of the unknown …
* leads us to spend our lives desperately trying to cushion ourselves in security,
* stops us from taking charge of our destiny,
* controls our lives and limits the choices we make.

The deep dark emotional centre of my fear is a fear of failure. This is far more powerful and all consuming than the actual fear of losing your job. It's built up of internal demons that drive your fear and constantly play on your psyche, wearing you down day after day.

How often have you asked yourself, 'Why me? What's wrong with me?' 'What will everyone think of me? I'll never be a success!' or simply felt, 'I'm not good enough!' Or maybe your worry is about who you'll be letting down, how you'll ever find the time, or how to juggle your work with family life and running a home. Whatever your particular fear, it helps to remember you're not the only one to feel like this. It's quite normal to feel afraid, and even the most successful people doubt themselves sometimes before, during and long after they've made it.

No matter who you are, or what you do, we are all governed by our emotional demons – and these can be more crippling than the fear itself.

When you're flying high your demons seem so far away, but when you wake up at the bottom of a pit you need a demon-busting strategy in place to dig yourself out. It's harder sometimes than others.

It's vitally important to clearly identify the demons driving your fear. The better you're able to pinpoint them, the easier it is to tackle each and every one of them head on. This will ultimately break down the overriding force your fears hold over you.

DEMON BUSTING

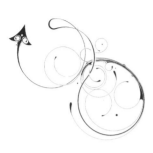

Fear is, in essence, an intangible force, and demons are the elements driving that force. I have an overriding fear of failure, but the demons driving my fear, giving it momentum and velocity include:

★ What will other people think?
  ★ Everyone will think you're a loser
  ★ No one will like you
  ★ They'll all nod their heads and smirk 'I told you so'
★ How will I survive?
  ★ You could lose everything
★ My career will be over.
  ★ What career? You never had one. So no surprise there!
  ★ You simply don't have what it takes to get to the top
  ★ You'll always be jack of all trades but master of none
★ I'll never succeed.
  ★ Well you haven't exactly got a track record to prove otherwise
  ★ The sooner you accept your lot in life, the happier you'll be
★ I'm not good enough.
  ★ You're not intelligent enough
  ★ You've made too many wrong choices, your career's in tatters.
  You've missed the boat.

It's a miracle I get out of bed in the morning, and yet people tell me I seem so confident. In truth, I am confident but that's only because I've learnt how to keep my demons at bay. Every time one of my demons starts sniggering in my ear, I'm ready and armed to fight it off. Here are some of my demon-busting strategies:

MY DEMONS	MY VOICE OF DEMON DESTRUCTION
Everyone will think you're a loser	Great! If they'd like to point out what I've lost I might be able to find it a bit quicker
What will other people think?	How should I know? I'm not a mind-reader
No one will like you	That's a little dramatic, don't you think? I have evidence to prove otherwise
They'll all smirk – 'I Told You So'	Since when did you get so good at predicting the future?
You could lose everything	This is true, but at least I'll have a story to tell
How will you survive?	Heard of the A-Team? I'll make a plan
You simply don't have what it takes	Did I ask for your opinion? Last time I looked you didn't have much to offer beyond your big blabbermouth either!
You're not intelligent enough	Since when did brains have anything to do with success?
You'll never succeed	No? And what exactly have you achieved lately?

BE YOURSELF

I remember once, one of my boyfriends told me I'd never get anywhere in life because I'm so emotional. Well, he was wrong. We are what we are and trying to be what we're not can be totally draining. There's nothing wrong with being emotional; you simply need to channel it in the right direction by doing something creative instead of destructive. Or just take a break from life for a while and do something completely different. You know yourself and your strengths better than anyone else, so don't let other people's negativity or the demons in your mind penetrate your soul.

DEMON MANAGEMENT

Once you've identified the demons driving your fear, it's much easier to tackle them individually and develop a demon-management strategy. At various stages during the last five years I've hit a number of brick walls and devised various strategies to help me chip away at my wall of fear and eventually break through.

To give you an idea, this is a demon-busting strategy I wrote for myself in January 2002 when I'd been self-employed for a year and was really struggling with committing to my dream. The fear of failure was all-consuming and paralysing at times.

EMOTIONAL SURVIVAL PLAN FOR NICKY HAMBLETON-JONES AKA MS TRAMP2VAMP

1 *Survival plan for the good times*
★ Wake up at 8 a.m., unless I have an important meeting scheduled
★ Make breakfast and drink coffee until 8.30 a.m.
★ Spend half an hour devising plan of action for the day – 9 a.m.
★ 9.00 a.m. shower and get dressed
★ 9.30 –11 a.m. return emails and do immediate tasks
★ 11–1 p.m. Get creative – have a mini brainstorm. Think of five goals you'd like to achieve and put an action plan in place for each, aim to achieve two of them by the end of the week – so keep them simple.
★ 1 p.m. lunch and take a walk to focus mind on afternoon's tasks
★ Schedule all meetings from 2 p.m. to 5.30 p.m.
★ If no meetings scheduled do one of the following (these afternoons can be spent out in 'exotic' locations such as coffee shops):
a Spend one to two afternoons a week reviewing marketing activity and plan, following up on outstanding tasks, etc.
b Spend one afternoon a week sorting out admin.
c Spend one afternoon a week doing something inspirational, e.g. going shopping, reading fashion magazines, watching fashion TV
d Spend one afternoon a week being creative, remind myself of my dream and consolidate vision
★ Go to gym 5.30–7 p.m.

2 *Survival plan for when disaster (heartbreak, a major setback at work) strikes*

★ Follow plan of action for a good day until 12 midday, then spend rest of day treating myself and feeling good that I got the important things done
★ Have hot bubble bath, watch a trashy film or read a favourite novel
★ Go to gym from 5.30 to 7 p.m.
★ Try to meet up with a friend at 7.30 p.m.
★ Make a list of five good things that happened to me today
★ Feel fantastic sense of relief when I get into bed that the day is over, never to be repeated, and trust that tomorrow will be better

Lesson Learned: I always recover. Don't fight the bad times; instead try to enjoy the time I need to heal my heart and soul so I can embrace the opportunities that are waiting for me. Keep surrendering to the Universe and simply give in on life and love in general. Things always get better … but never, ever give up my dream … always keep believing.

BE KIND TO YOURSELF

My most effective demon-busting strategy in those early days was to simply cop out and do something totally different. Don't forget that, when you're putting yourself through a process of change, it's extremely taxing emotionally and physically, and sometimes your brain just can't process everything fast enough, which is when it can all become overwhelming and your fears take hold. It's at this point that you need to stop and have a complete break – and look for inspiration or ideas in different places. Spend time with friends or your children. Children have a wonderful way of taking you out of your reality and making you laugh. I would often spend time with a good friend of mine's twins when I needed to switch off and give myself a mental break for an afternoon. After a day or two (or – in extreme cases – three), you usually feel much better and able to tackle the challenges that lie ahead with renewed vigour.

I like to think of it as the 'winter' of change. There are times for energy and activity and there are times when we need to stop and take stock – giving our body and soul the opportunity to renew and restore. Remember this is a journey and there's no knowing how long the road to success will be, so what's the point running yourself into the ground, when you'll be no use to anyone? Time to regroup is as important as time for action. It's the down time that helps define the direction you need to take.

THE LIGHT AT THE END OF THE TUNNEL

My experience of fear is that it never totally goes away, but you get better at managing it. The further along the journey you go, the higher the stakes and the bigger the fear can get. By understanding what drives your fear, you have a better chance of dealing with it.

Now that I have a successful business and TV show, I still have fears, and my demons haven't disappeared, but they're just not as powerful as they used to be, they no longer control me – I'm in control of them.

The only thing that can really fight fear is a rock-solid belief in yourself and your dream. You need to be completely certain before embarking on your change journey that this is something you really want to do – otherwise your fear will eventually suffocate your dream, your passion and your opportunity to be different and stand out in the crowd. You will become an empty vessel that goes through life wondering, 'What if?', but you'll never find out.

And when the going gets tough and you start to falter, go back to your dream and remember why you started out on this programme for change in the first place. Dig out that wish list and revisit your intentions. Look back over the past few months and acknowledge just how far you've come. Call on your dream team for moral support and to have fun. Think positively about everything you have going for you. Face down your fears and, if you need to, put your own demon-busting strategy into action – or follow mine. Trust me, you'll get through the tough times and will be even stronger as a result.

If you follow these simple principles – whether you decide to change your job, lose weight, get fit or revamp your look – I can assure you that not only will you succeed, but you'll never look back. Time for a new you!

CHAPTER THREE

Take a look
at yourself

'THERE ARE NO LIMITS TO WHAT YOU CAN ACHIEVE WHEN YOU FEEL GOOD ABOUT YOURSELF.' **ANON**

What does how you look have to do with changing your life? The answer is everything! Whatever it is you're trying to achieve, from changes in your personal life to your career, the way you look and present yourself will play a large part in how successful you are. This is obviously a subject that's close to my heart and draws directly on my own passion for style. I think it's a great place to start the process of change and, what's more, simple improvements to your appearance are easily achievable and immediate, while changing your career or dropping a dress size can take a lot longer. Take a moment to reread the opening quote. I firmly believe if you feel confident in the way you're presenting yourself to the world, you can do or be anything you want.

The first steps are easy. I will help you identify your best features (yes, you do have them!), to put together your personal wish list and practical intentions for the way you want to look, from your head to your toes, working on your hair, make-up, body and beauty routine. Even you will be impressed by the time I've finished with you!

First impressions
How long do you think you have to create that all-important great first impression? Whatever your answer, you're probably wrong, because it actually takes just one-tenth of a second – and this particularly applies to impressions of attractiveness and trustworthiness. US psychologist Alex Todorov came up with the figure after a series of experiments carried out at Princeton University.

take a look at yourself

Looking good makes you feel so much better, and it even helps you ride out the bad times. I remember when I went through my spate of redundancies it became really embarrassing when every time I bumped into old friends I was always unemployed. I was so determined that no one would feel sorry for me that I took control of the only thing I could – the way I looked. I made sure that no matter how tough life got, no one could ever tell unless they knew me really well.

I always made sure I was in shape and well groomed. Keeping trim and fit didn't have to cost money, and I got very creative with the way I dressed, so I looked good even if it wasn't high fashion. I do believe it's one of my most effective survival strategies. If your life is falling apart, you've gained weight as a result, and your despair is written all over your face – the last thing you'll want to do is go out and mingle with other people. All you want to do is stay put and wallow some more and it becomes a vicious circle.

MY 'LOVE THEORY'

The way you feel about yourself impacts the opportunities that cross your path. I refer to this as my 'love theory'. When you fall in love, everything comes up roses. All of a sudden you find that extra half an hour to decide what to wear in the morning. Keeping yourself groomed is effortless and you simply wouldn't dream of going a day without clean hair. All the things we're constantly moaning that we never have time to do seem easy – proving it's not a lack of time but a lack of motivation. What are your priorities? Our lives are a direct reflection of the choices we make every day. So if you're not looking your best, the chances are it's because you've chosen not to give your appearance the attention it deserves.

Perhaps I'm being a little harsh, but we all have those days when we get out of the wrong side of the bed and, no matter how hard we try, nothing seems to go right. This is because our state of mind and the vibes we give off directly influence the energy we attract. If you're in a negative mind-set you're more likely to attract negativity; if you're in a positive mood you'll attract good things. This might sound a bit generalist, but time and time again I prove myself right. The most challenging thing is recognising your power to attract good or bad and your power to switch your luck from bad to brilliant.

ONE OF A KIND

Think about it, you are utterly unique and that's what makes you special. So why is it that most of us don't capitalise on our biggest asset – which is our difference – and instead spend our lives trying to look like our best friend, our favourite celebrity, or whatever we think society expects of us? As a result, we simply end up looking like a second-rate version of someone else instead of a first-rate version of ourselves – a clone when we should be the original. Have you noticed that a bunch of girls who hang about together often start to look the same? Take a look around you next time you go to book club or your weekly coffee morning. How many women really stand out? Ask yourself – do you?

'IF YOU WANT PEOPLE TO NOTICE YOU, BE YOURSELF.'
MAX CLIFFORD

CALL ON YOUR DREAM TEAM

This is the ideal moment to call for backup. I want you to try something for me. Ask a friend you can trust, or a close family member, to describe the way you look. What are your defining features? Then ask a boyfriend or your partner the same question, as well as what made them fall for you in the first place. Reflect and ask yourself whether you're making the most of your best assets? Perhaps your legs are no longer in good shape, perhaps your teeth have become discoloured so that your smile no longer sparkles or your hair tone drains the colour from your eyes.

Ask a friend:
★ How would you describe me?
★ What features stand out? Good and bad.
★ How would you describe my style?
★ Does my style reflect my personality?
★ What did you notice first about me?
★ What do I need to change or work on?

You can actually do this for each other. It works best if you apply the questions to physical features, personality and style as a complete package. You'll probably be surprised at what you find out. It may make you feel uncomfortable and you may not like all the answers, but if it's done in a positive context it's sometimes good to get a reality check.

Getting feedback enables you to build up a picture of how other people see you and helps you identify what you need to work on most. And unless you're happy settling for second best, now's the perfect time to assess the reasons why you let yourself go in the first place. What's holding you back, preventing you from creating a first-rate version of yourself?

STOP telling yourself:
★ I'm too old
★ Too tired
★ Have too little time
★ No money
★ I will when I've lost those extra pounds
★ When the children are older
★ It's not important

Excuses, excuses, excuses …it's what we fill our lives with every day. Reasons why we can't or won't, instead of when or how. I believe each and every one of us has the potential to look good now – no matter what our age, shape or stage of life. Yes, it may take a bit of effort, but it could change the way you feel about yourself and the way other people, including your partner, react to you. It could reignite a flame that you thought had been extinguished; it might even help you get that promotion you've always wanted.

REINVENT YOURSELF

'I BELIEVE THAT ONE DEFINES ONESELF BY REINVENTION. TO NOT BE LIKE YOUR PARENTS. TO NOT BE LIKE YOUR FRIENDS. TO BE YOURSELF. TO CUT YOURSELF OUT OF STONE.' **HENRY ROLLINS**

Just as products have to be constantly changed and relaunched to survive in a competitive marketplace, so do we. I want you to try to think of yourself like a product – mascara, for example. There are countless varieties of mascara out there, each of them essentially performing the same task, which is to give your lashes impact – whether it's lengthening, thickening or darkening. Ultimately we wear mascara to make our eyes look more defined and dramatic, but what differentiates one mascara from the next?

The key to success lies in the point of difference one product has over another. In the same way, in our ever more crowded society, competition for boys, toys and success is becoming more and more challenging as the stakes get higher. Fortunately you are an individual, which gives you a natural point of difference, but you need to capitalise on this and cultivate your 'stand-out' factor. At the moment you're just blending into the background. You want people to wake up and take notice of just how fabulous you really are.

take a look at yourself

WHAT'S YOUR TDF ('TO DIE FOR') FACTOR?

Just as products have a Unique selling Point, so do we. I like to refer to this as your TDF, which stands for 'to die for', factor. It's the one thing that you have that other people would kill for – the one thing that others envy most about you. Think of the feedback your close friends and family gave you as to your most defining features. This will help you identify and make the most of your own personal TDF factor, which is a key step towards reinventing yourself.

I thought it would be interesting to try out a little research on a group of my friends. Here are some of the different TDF factors they identified in one another:

'Bohemian style and voluptuousness.'

'Hippy, beatnik chic. She always makes the most of herself.'

'Height and elegance.'

'Warm smile which makes her seem friendly and approachable.'

'Full of Eastern promise – when dressed to go out.'

'Great legs.'

'Unerring sense of style.'

'Gorgeous pre-Raphaelite hair.'

'Arty, quirky dress sense which reflects her personality.'

'Colourful, vibrant and flamboyant.'

Interestingly, more of the comments referred to style and whether or not a person made the most of herself than they did to particular physical features. Which, if you think about it, is great news, as all of us can improve our style and learn to enhance our best features.

DISCOVERING A NEW YOU

Take Madonna, for example. As fabulous as she may look, before she launches a new album she always reinvents the way she looks, so ensuring she's constantly setting – rather than following – trends.

Now imagine a group of people are discussing how to relaunch or reinvent you. They'd run through all your positive attributes and then they'd discuss what needs to be done to make you a more dynamic, improved version of yourself while at the same time capitalising on and making the most of your TDF factor.

In other words, what about you is a little rusty, outdated, or simply no longer has the appeal it once did? This is where you really need to be honest with yourself and take a critical view of the way other people see you, and I'm not just talking about your clothes here – remember to think of yourself as a whole package.

Be self-aware
★ Take time to study yourself in a mirror.
★ Look at the way you move and your body language.
★ What facial expressions do you pull when you're talking?
★ How do you walk? Do you walk tall and confidently, do you slouch, do you stomp, or perhaps you sashay sexily? Ask yourself how you would like to look when you walk – and practise!
★ Remember other people take just one-tenth of a second to form a first impression of you.
★ Don't rush into a room full of people. Pause at the entrance to create an impression.

YOUR TOP-TO-TOE GUIDE TO A NEW YOU

People always ask me what makes the biggest difference when transforming someone. I believe it's not just one thing: it's the whole package. You can wear fashionable clothes but if your hairstyle's old-fashioned and dowdy you'll still look frumpy. To completely transform yourself you have to pay attention to every detail.

HAIR FLAIR

So many of us underestimate how important hair is to the overall impression we make. Think about it, when you meet someone new, you'll often forget their name but you'll always remember their hair colour. Or when we describe a friend or loved one we start off with their hair. She's got long dark brown hair, or short blonde hair, or curly red hair. Immediately an image of that person comes to mind. Your hair makes such a visual impact on other people it's important to invest time in creating a look that makes you feel good and gives you impact. Mousy brown will never cut it in the sex appeal stakes. It's time to consider whether your hair's actually doing anything for you.

★ When did you last change your hairstyle?
★ When did you last change your hair colour? I don't just mean having your roots done, I mean dramatically change your colour?
★ Does your hair look glossy and shiny?
★ Do people comment on your hair?
★ Do you actually like the way it looks?
★ Do you colour your hair?
★ When did you last change your hairdresser?
★ When did you last ask your hairdresser what he thinks you should do with your hair?

If you answered No, Never or Can't remember to more than two of the above, you and I need to have a little talk. My friend, it's time to change your headdress and make more of your crowning glory.
Now, this isn't my expertise, so I'm going to pop over to my friend AB (more commonly known as Andrew Barton), fabulous hairdresser extraordinaire, who is so booked up these days you need to be dating Prince William to get an appointment.

ASK THE EXPERT

★ **Andrew, why is hair so important?**
Hair's important because it's part of a woman's identity and personality. It's a real fashion tool, something she can play with through the seasons and different stages of her life.

★ **Do you think there is such a thing as finding your perfect hairstylist?**
I think in the pursuit of finding the perfect hairstylist, one you feel comfortable and confident with, it is worth getting a lot of opinions. Shop around for at least three consultations at different salons. Find the person you feel comfortable with, who understands you as a person and the look you want to achieve.

I think you tend to build up a relationship with your hairdresser and together you find out what works and what doesn't work, so it can be a good idea to stay with the same one. But there are some hairdressers who are guilty of assuming a client doesn't want to change their style. A good hairdresser will keep changing and adapting someone's hair anyway, whether it's through colour, shape or the way they blow-dry it.

★ **What do you think about grey hair?**
I think grey hair on women is ageing, colourless and tends to make you look drab. There's a very small percentage of women who look really good with grey hair, but it depends on the hair texture and density. If it's coarse and wiry then it's not attractive. If it's very sleek, smooth and shiny then you might be able to get away with it. It also depends on skin tone and eye colour. If someone has pale skin and grey-blue eyes, sometimes grey hair can work for them. Grey hair isn't a no-no for everybody, but for most people it'll age them by ten years.

★ **What do you think is the most versatile length for a woman?**
I'm a great believer that hair should be one thing or another. It should either be above the shoulders or below. As soon as it starts hitting the shoulders, it doesn't matter how well it's cut, it will be neither one thing nor the other. There's a lot of versatility with having length in the hair because you can tie it up, tie it back, wear it down and it's easier to create different textures – either curl, wave or straight. If it's short you are stuck with one look and it's not that versatile to play with.

★ **What's the easiest way to update your look?**
Colour. Colour can give you a dramatic change; it can give you the colour of the season or completely change your

take a look at yourself

personality. In the 1970s and 1980s women used colour to cover grey hair; today it's a real accessory to fashion. It's an easy way to change hair and isn't a massive commitment – you can always change it back or into something different.

★ **What can you do with superfine hair?**
If you want to create body and inject volume, the best things are heated rollers. This is quite an old-fashioned tool but it's making a big comeback now for hairdressers. It tends to give the hair more long-lasting support than a blow-dry which is quite difficult to do as you are manipulating two hands, the hairdryer in one and a brush in the other. And keep it short, or above shoulder length, so it's actually doing something and you can see a definite line in the haircut. If it's well cut into a shape you've got much more of a chance of managing and controlling it.

★ **What can you do with super-thick hair?**
There's quite a lot you can do with super-thick hair. There are hair-cutting techniques where you can disconnect layers of hair, reducing the thickness on the underneath but still keeping length on the top – it's almost like putting hair on a diet. If you've got curly, wavy hair that expands to make the hair look even thicker, there are straightening systems that you can use to relax the hair which last up to about three months. These help to make it sit closer to the head, but it doesn't have to be poker straight.

★ **What about wild curly hair?**
That's all about using the right products. Modern straightening products are quite lubricating on the hair, which help to weigh the curl down, reducing its bounce.

★ **How often should you update your look?**
I think every season is probably too much. Hair fashion doesn't move that quickly; for example, fringes have been quite a fashion statement for a while now. But I think every few years people need to start thinking of adapting their style. Sometimes it's a question of tweaking it every few months to adapt the shape. Often women find a shape that works for them, so if you're a bob girl, and a bob works, stay with it but keep tweaking it: the volume, length, shape, fringe, etc. Woman today are more confident with doing their hair at home and adapting it to suit different looks.

★ **What's the biggest mistake people make with their hair as they get older?**
I think one mistake is that they get stuck in a rut and wear the same hairstyle that

worked for them twenty years ago. Secondly, they look back and try to emulate the time in their lives when they felt they looked their best. They get stuck in the past and don't update their style and move it on. A good hairdresser can help with this.

On a personal note:

★ **How did you get to the position you are in now?**

I'm from a small mining town and although that stood me in really good stead as an apprentice, I was never going to fully understand the world of hairdressing there – so travel's really helped. I worked in the US, Australia and spent a long time in London. I think that international experience has definitely helped me understand women and hair. I've also worked with some great people over the years. I'm not saying it's all about contacts, but it's good to put yourself in places where you're going to learn – and I'm still learning. It's an essential part of career development. The minute you stop learning, is when you start to stagnate.

★ **What sets you apart?**

I'd like to think I'm pretty down to earth with no airs and graces. What you see is what you get. I care very much about the industry and how it's represented. It's not all about me, me, me and ego, ego, ego. I'd like to think I'm very approachable and easy to work with. Hopefully, people I work with respect me as well.

★ **What's the secret of your success?**

A combination of teamwork, drive and passion. And you need a really good foundation and training. My first boss taught me all the old-fashioned disciplines of finger waving and roller setting, which have really stood me in good stead. There are a lot of hairdressers who can only pinpoint their work to a particular era or decade.

Training is right at the foundation of it. Then passion. It's hard work and long hours which can be draining emotionally and mentally, but that is what creates the success – perseverance and determination. Hard work is part of a Yorkshireman's philosophy. The best compliment you can pay a Yorkshireman is that he's a hard worker. I'd hope that's what everyone would say about me.

★ **What's your TDF factor?**

I think it's the fact that I'm successful but really down to earth and real. When I first came to London, I purposefully tried to change my accent but then I realised it just wasn't me. My accent is part of my character and who I am.

rlfriend – so now you're in the *know* and there's no
...se for tired, dull, boring hair. I want you to go out and
make an appointment with a hairdresser by the end of the week.
Then just sit back and wait for the world to notice and the
compliments to roll in…now doesn't that feel good?

But don't think you can rest on your laurels just yet. Our work
is far from finished.

MAKE-UP MAGIC

Your hair is now the envy of the neighbourhood, but does your make-
up still leave much to be desired? You probably think it's fine, but
'fine' isn't enough when we're aiming for 'fabulous'. Ask yourself this:

★ Do you actually wear make-up?
★ When did you last update the products and colours you use?
★ When did you last update your foundation?
★ Do you wear sun protection every day?
★ How often do you change your mascara?
★ Do you know how to apply make-up to best enhance your features?
★ And how to hide your worst features?

If you've answered, Nope, Not often, Sometimes, Never thought about
it, we've got some work to do. If you're part of the fresh-faced brigade
then I'm not suggesting you need to start painting your face to the
nines. On the contrary, make-up should be all about helping you feel
good about yourself, making the most of your assets and giving you
the confidence you need to go out there and show the world just how
wonderful you are.

This is another occasion when we could all do with a little extra
help, so I'm going to ask make-up diva to the stars, Ruby Hammer, for
her trade secrets on how to look gorgeous, rain or shine. She certainly
does, so she must be doing something right.

ASK THE EXPERT

★ **Ruby, do you think make-up can transform anyone from beast to beauty?**
I think everyone looks better with make-up. Even top models don't always look great when they wake up in the morning. Thank goodness we have a choice of products to enable us to make the best of ourselves.

★ **When you're making over someone, what's the first thing you do?**
Before anything else, I analyse a face to see where the problem areas lie. You can't just use your favourite products over and over again; you have to think about what's going to work for this person.

★ **What are the key elements of any make-up routine?**
There are three key factors. People think of make-up as colour, but it's more than that. It's also about the texture of the product and the tools with which you apply it. For instance, a liquid eyeliner, by its very nature, is going be darker and more intense than a pencil.

Secondly, people tend to ignore the tools when they buy make-up. They focus on the eye shadow but don't think about how they're going to apply it. You need the proper tools, like a good set of brushes for a start.

Thirdly, people always try to copy what looks good on someone else, when they should be thinking, how will this work on me? You can only find out by experimenting on your own face.

How do you create ...?
★ **Gorgeous eyes**
It's crucial not to overwhelm your eyes so that all people see is your eye make-up. Try to emphasise their shape and colour. The key is mascara. It opens your eyes and transforms their shape and your whole look. But be careful with the application – too much can look cheap.

★ **Luscious lips**
Remember to moisturise your lips first to give a smooth foundation. Always use a lip liner to define the contours, but that doesn't have to be a hard, dark line. It can be transparent or blend with your lipstick. Then add your favourite lip colour and a little gloss on your lower lip just below the cupid's bow on your upper lip. Or place a dab of pearly iridescent lip gloss on those areas to create the optical illusion of plump, luscious lips.

★ **Cheekbones**
There is no one right way to apply blusher. It all depends on your face shape. If you have strong cheekbones all you need to do

take a look at yourself

is follow the bones with a bit of blush. If you naturally have a round face, applying blush on the apples of your cheeks makes it look fuller, but applying it on the diagonal is more flattering and will slim down your face.

For a more natural daytime look, you should apply a little blusher on the apples of your cheeks. Alternatively, for a more sophisticated look in the evening, applying blusher on the diagonal below your cheekbones helps contour them.

As we get older we lose a lot of our cheek volume, so applying blusher on the apples of your cheeks looks younger and fresher.

★ Flawless skin

It's very easy to achieve a flawless skin depending on how much product you're prepared to wear. The quality of your natural skin will determine the weight of product you should use and where you need it. In the same way we all wear a bra to give a good line under clothes but we all choose different bras depending on our shape and the occasion. The same principle applies to foundation – everyone is different and therefore one product, no matter how good, won't work for all.

How do you disguise ...?
★ Less than perfect complexions

This is nothing to do with age; it's to do with the quality of your skin. I'm amazed that in the twenty years I've been working, people still shy away from using concealers. A perfect example is Yves Saint Laurent Touche Éclat – everybody has one of these in their make-up bag which they think of as a concealer. But it is not a concealer; it's a light-diffusing reflector. A good concealer can be a girl's best weapon, but so many women don't take advantage of this fantastic tool. You can get away without wearing foundation but you can't get away without a concealer. If push came to shove, and I lost my whole make-up kit but had my concealers with me, I could still transform a whole face. It doesn't work with foundation alone – skin never looks as polished or finished as with a concealer.

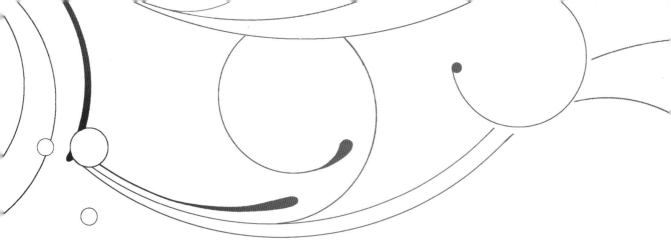

★ **Prominent noses**

Bar having surgery it's very difficult. Either you make friends with it or draw attention away from it by emphasising another part of your face – your eyes, skin or lips. Using make-up to contour the nose by highlighting the centre and shading the sides only really works in photos.

★ **How do you define a jawline?**

You can use a darker powder around your jawline to define it, but again this technique is best used for photos. If you want to use make-up, make sure you blend it properly, otherwise it will just look as though you haven't washed. Good posture can do wonders for your jawline.

★ **How long should we spend on our make-up every day?**

That depends on how much time you've got! If you want to pull off something quite spectacular like fabulous bold lips or dramatic eyes, false eyelashes, or eyeliner, it's good to give yourself enough time to fix any mistakes. However, if you're going to work and you have the right tools and products, you can do it in as little as five minutes. A multi-way product, lip balm, concealer and mascara is all you really need. I would say that fifteen minutes is ideal as it gives your make-up a chance to settle.

Tip: Make sure you leave enough time for your moisturiser to sink in before applying your make-up. This will give you a better finish, which lasts longer.

One of the common mistakes people make is that they either don't moisturise first and apply make-up onto dry, patchy skin, or they use too much moisturiser, which means any make-up slides off the face.

★ **How often should we change our make-up routine?**

I think there's always something to be said for 'if it isn't broke, why fix it?' but I also think make-up by its very nature is quite frivolous and fashion directed.

take a look at yourself

Everybody has certain things they always fall back on, but there will be times where you feel like you're in a rut and everyone else looks fresher. Then it's worth revisiting what you use and how you apply it.

★ **What's the quickest way to take your day look into the evening?**
You already know what colours work for you in the day, so it's just a question of adding a little more. This is what I do:
1 Take off your lipstick and apply lip balm to moisturise your lips.
2 Comb through your eyelashes.
3 Blot and repair your foundation where necessary.
4 Then reapply the same products over your existing make-up, with a slightly stronger hand, or add a few extras like an eyeliner or a lip gloss. You don't need to start from scratch.

On a personal note:
★ **What's it like being Ruby Hammer?**
Most women have to juggle a career, relationship, children and friends, and at different times of your life you have different priorities. I've always tried to do what feels right in my heart. In terms of work I've always chosen to do things I enjoy, my way. I love what I'm doing now. I started off studying economics and ended up in make-up. My love and passion for what I do is what's brought me success. It hasn't all been easy, I've had to work at it, and I still do. In a freelance world, you're only as good as your last job. I never stop trying to better myself – the day you do is the day your career is over. Never become complacent.

★ **What does it take to get to the top?**
You need to be tenacious – if you're a quitter, you won't get anywhere in life. When an opportunity arises which feels right, just go for it and see what happens.

★ **What's your TDF?**
I think it's the fact that I look young for my age. I've just been lucky with my genes and I look after myself and it shows. I also don't try to hide my age.

★ **If there was one thing you'd like to change about yourself, what would it be?**
My saddlebags! Generally I've got my dad's figure but then I've got these saddlebags which are my mum's signature. Since the age of sixteen I've been self-conscious about them and would love to get rid of them …oh, and perhaps a bit more hair. Mine is very thin and sparse in places.

So there you have it: even gorgeous girls like Ruby don't think they're perfect – there's a glimmer of hope for the rest of us!

Ruby's given you her pearls of wisdom, now it's up to you to put her tips into practice. But buying make-up can be a daunting task. One glance around the beauty hall of any department store confronts you with a sea of choices. So where do you begin?

A little know-how

★ It may sound simplistic, but the packaging and ethos of certain brands will appeal to you more than others. Start with those.

★ Many brands offer free makeovers and their trained assistants can give you excellent advice. Alternatively, book yourself a one-to-one session with a make-up artist in the privacy of your own home.

★ Don't be shy about asking for samples. It's much better to try products before you buy and in natural daylight.

★ At the same time, ask about application and how to use products for the best results.

★ If you're worried your make-up's outdated, keep your look fresh by scanning magazines for seasonal tips.

★ Ask friends whose make-up you like what they use or recommend.

★ Go for a makeover with a friend. You'll feel pampered, it's fun and, on a practical note, seeing how someone else is transformed can give you ideas.

★ Every six months, overhaul your make-up bag and throw out anything old, half-used or past its use-by date. And don't be tempted to hold on to free samples that never suited you in the first place.

★ Owning too many products is just confusing. Everything in your make-up bag should be something you feel confident about and use regularly.

Well-shaped and well-defined eyebrows open up your eyes and give an instant face-lift.

Key kit: To maximise your eyelashes, always use an eyelash curler before sweeping on mascara.

BODY BEAUTIFUL

Before I even move on to your clothes, I need you to sort out a few things for me that will ultimately smooth the road to a stylish new you.

The time has come, darlings, to embrace your luscious curves and give yourself a little bit of loving, and by that I mean turning your body into the ultimate clotheshorse. Let's face it, when we feel depressed about our bodies we tend to neglect them even more. In fact, chances are we don't even look at ourselves naked in the mirror. We simply don't want to confront the reality, which is that you've let yourself go! Yip, let's just be brutal for a moment while we consider when you last had a bikini wax? A pedicure? A manicure? When you last buffed and polished your skin so it glowed? No time for pampering? Well, my friend, if you don't give your body a bit of loving, it's going to start looking neglected.

A new hairstyle and a new wardrobe can only do so much. At the end of the day, the devil's in the detail. Ever admired a Frenchwoman for her effortless elegance? I can assure you it probably wasn't just her clothes you took heed of, but the fact that her nails were beautifully groomed and her feet looked as if they'd been wrapped in silk booties all night they were so smooth. Not a stray hair visible anywhere on her body as you clomp past taking in your chipped nails and hairy toes. To truly carry off your clothes with style, you need to invest in secure foundations, which shouldn't break the bank.

In the early days, while establishing my business, I didn't have two cents to rub together, but I had to look as though I did. So to keep my head and body above water I devised my 'Beauty in a Flash' routine –

quick and easy with results to guarantee attention. Everything
I did was attached to a daily event so as not to require additional
scheduling, and it was always DIY so it didn't cost a fortune.

Beauty in a Flash
Daily routine:
★ When in the shower/bath, wash body with exfoliating body wash.
★ When brushing teeth, examine eyebrows and pluck any stray hairs.
★ After toning and moisturising your face, moisturise your body.
★ When in bed, file nails and rub cuticle oil into cuticles.
★ While on tube/train, apply nail polish.

Weekly routine:
★ On Sunday evenings, while watching your favourite movie, give
yourself a mini-facial (cleanse and exfoliate skin and apply hydrating
face mask).
★ Whilst waiting for face mask to develop, place feet in a bowl of
warm water and push back cuticles before trimming and reapplying
nail polish if required.
★ Once a week, apply a deep conditioning mask to your hair and
wrap in a hot towel for ten minutes before rinsing.

Monthly routine:
★ Book in for hair removal or go for the DIY option if you're
brave enough.
★ Touch up your hair colour while tidying the house. This only
takes thirty minutes if you're a dab hand like me, or book into
your favourite salon for the deluxe treatment.
★ Book in for a trim to avoid split, dry ends building up.

SCENT-SATIONAL YOU

Use fragrance to affect your makeover in a deliciously forceful manner. Smell has always been a primitive tactile sense, used to great effect over the ages and through the history of man and, more to the point, of woman. So, launch an intense search for your signature scent and take your time. Your nose will tell you when you've found it, and so will almost everyone you pass on the street! The trick is to find a scent that evokes your special essence. It could be floral, it could be citrusy and green, it could be mellow and fruity, it could be one loud and sexy exclamation. But it has to be YOU! And when you wear it, you should love the smell.

Choosing a scent

★ Don't confuse yourself by trying too many different scents at once. Your nose can only properly assess two or three at a time.

★ It's worth trying out completely new scents on perfume cards first, and then try the ones you like best on your skin.

★ Don't assume that because you love the smell of a particular perfume on someone else that it will smell the same on you. Perfumes smell slightly different on everyone because they're affected by your skin's acidity and natural chemistry.

★ Once you've found a scent that you think you like, try it out on your skin at least a couple of times to make sure you really do like it and can live with the smell.

★ Trying it out before buying also gives you an idea of how well the fragrance lasts on you. Again this will be affected by your skin's own chemical make-up.

★ Eau de toilette is the cheapest and most diluted version of a scent. Eau de parfum and pure perfume are more expensive because they are more intense and generally last longer.

★ The smell of a particular scent can also vary between eau de toilette, eau de parfum and perfume – don't assume you'll like the more expensive perfume just because you love the eau de toilette.

★ When choosing a scent, think about when you want to wear it. The intense perfume that makes you feel grown up and sexy on cold winter evenings can make you feel heavy and headachy on a bright summer's day.

★ For some people it works to have two different scents – one for day and one for evening, or seasonal for summer and winter.

Whatever you choose, make sure you wear your scent every day. It lifts your mood just as much as a new outfit or haircut and ensures you always smell distinct and delicious. Remember that the sense that most powerfully stimulates memory is the sense of smell, so don't neglect your perfume.

Be careful where you spray your perfume. The skin on the neck area is extremely thin and prone to redness as a reaction to perfume. Instead, spray on the inside of wrists or into the air and walk through the spray to dissipate the scent over your body, rather than concentrate on the décolletage.

ONE STEP AT A TIME

It's always easier to maintain a look than to create it from scratch. Letting yourself go completely makes the task of restoration seem insurmountable and time consuming – when it doesn't have to be. Even if you're not in perfect shape, grooming yourself will make you feel a stone lighter and it will also help you value and appreciate the beautiful body you have. Not only that, you'll look expensive.

Right, there you have it, no excuse not to have luscious locks and a perfect pout – whatever age, size or shape you are. Each and every one of us can do something to improve our hair and make-up, right? You'll be amazed at how much better you'll start to feel.

Next up … yip, you guessed it: time to dive through those wardrobe doors and unleash those demons … Can't wait!

Style-wise

CHAPTER FOUR

'STYLE IS KNOWING WHO YOU ARE, WHAT YOU WANT TO SAY AND NOT GIVING A DAMN.' **GORE VIDAL**

Now that we've sorted out your hair, face and body, it's time to move on to those strips of fabric you use as an excuse to cover up. Before we do, I'd like you to complete the following questionnaire so we all know what we're dealing with. I want you to really think about your answers and evaluate yourself through the eyes of others. Or, even better, imagine I'm standing in your bedroom right now, giving you the once over through my specs! Oh yes – it's reality-check time.

ARE YOU A TRAMP OR A VAMP?

Complete this 15-point assessment to discover whether you are
a Tramp or a Vamp? A = Yes, B = No, C = Sometimes

1 Do you believe you can enhance the way you look and feel every
day, with style? A B C
2 Do you only wear sexy underwear? A B C
3 Are you usually the life and soul of the party? A B C
4 Do you feel confident and sexy in all the clothes you wear? A B C
5 Do you have an outfit for every occasion? A B C
6 Do you feel comfortable about your size and the way you look? A B C
7 Do you always buy the latest fashions each season? A B C
8 Do you have a minimum of five handbags? A B C
9 Do you clear out your wardrobe regularly and only keep clothes that
fit you perfectly and make you feel fantastic? A B C
10 Do you wear high heels? A B C
11 Do you love to experiment with new looks and make a fashion
statement? A B C
12 Do you feel confident knowing what styles and colours suit you best? A B C
13 Do your friends often comment on the clothes you wear? A B C
14 Do you find shopping a fun, enjoyable pastime? A B C
15 Do you love living life? A B C

Scoring:
A = 3 points, B = 1 point, C = 2 points
Add up all your As, Bs and Cs to find out just how much of a tramp
or vamp you really are.

Is your score between 35 and 45?

Congratulations, you are a Vamp! A Vamp is someone who feels great on the inside and looks to die for on the outside. Someone who is in control of their lives and knows how to live and love life. A Vamp knows how to look fantastic, but is in touch with her inner self and knows how to make herself feel good on the inside too. She makes personal time to exercise, and pamper herself, because she understands how valuable she is. And can I just say, by Vamp I don't mean tart – I mean cool, sexy and confident.

Is your score between 16 and 34?

You have the potential to be a Vamp, but need to concentrate on building confidence and self-esteem. You know what suits you but you lack the confidence to try something new. You tend to opt for the safe option which looks OK, but you never stand out in the crowd. You need to start off by making more time for yourself and enlisting the help of a personal stylist or a very good friend who can coax you out of your comfort zone. Or simply read on and I'll share some of my trade secrets with you.

Is your score between 1 and 15?

Oops, you are a 'Tramp'! No, don't even bother looking in the mirror. Believe me when I tell you that you need an overhaul. A totally new look, a brand-new image that will open doors that you haven't seen yet, will rejuvenate you in a million little energising, simply cool ways. You will once again feel a tingle down your spine. The end result: YOU – but an enhanced, improved version of yourself. You have nothing to lose and everything to gain. Let's get to work!

goals, dreams and intentions

So there you have it, de-tramped and ready for an overhaul. Now, remember this isn't about following a strict set of rules. This is about creating a totally new and improved you; but before we get to the fun part we need to clear out the demons in your closet. Sorry sweetie, but they've simply got to go!

CLOSET SECRETS

We all have them, that pair of jeans you haven't been able to fit into for ten years but live in hope that some day you miraculously will. That horrific jumper your mother-in-law gave you for Christmas that you feel compelled to keep in case she pops round for tea. Our cupboards are full of secrets, past loves and past lives. Now's the time to move on and start living for the moment.

YOUR ESSENTIAL 'DE-CLOSET' GUIDE:

1 Bin your Fat clothes. If you put on weight you should look for a solution at the gym, not in your wardrobe.

2 What's the point of Thin clothes? Only keep clothes that fit you. No point in holding on to unrealistic reminders that will only serve to depress you further. Besides, fashion moves on at such a pace that even if you do reach your target weight they won't do you the justice your new-found figure deserves.

3 Ghastly gifts – who needs them? I know they were meant with the best intentions, but if you're not going to wear them, someone else might. You can always blame it on fashion.

4 At the end of a season, cull anything you haven't worn. Chances are it won't get a look-in next year either.

5 At the beginning of a season, remove anything that doesn't fit, is outdated or unlikely to be worn.

6 Nostalgic keepsakes. No point in holding on to the dress you wore on your honeymoon if you're no longer married – and the same goes for your ex's T-shirt. Your wardrobe needs to move on and so do you.

7 It cost you a fortune. Sell it to a second-hand shop. It's not adding value to your life if you no longer wear it.

8 We all make mistakes, so who needs reminding of them? Clear your conscience.

9 Lifestyle leftovers. No point having a wardrobe full of suits if you're now a full-time mum. Start fresh with a wardrobe that really works for you.

10 If it needs altering, fixing or cleaning, get it done or give it to someone who will.

Yip, you've got to be cruel to be kind. Shedding the demons in your closet is never an easy thing, but you will feel liberated once you have. Not only will you be able to see the wood for the trees, but your closet will be cleansed of any of those negative messages that drag you down every time you get dressed in the morning. You're single, you're too thin, you're too fat, you've got nothing to wear: guilt, hurt, disappointment. Take control of your wardrobe and you'll feel like a different person in no time.

BUILDING YOUR IDEAL WARDROBE

Now you've addressed the demons in your closet and know what's just got to go, at last you have the space to begin rebuilding. A fresh start to create a wardrobe that works for you and the life you lead, all year round and for any occasion from school sports day to high-powered business meetings and relaxed evenings out with friends.

There's nothing like beginning with the basics, and what's going on underneath the surface is every bit as important as the top coat. So let's first look at the secrets lurking in your underwear drawer before moving upwards and onwards.

BRA BASICS

Get yourself measured regularly. Breasts change shape and size throughout your life so don't just assume you're still wearing the right size bra. A well-fitted bra makes all the difference to the way your clothes look. It gives you support, and can make you look slimmer by lifting your boobs off your stomach, which will help to define your waist. Never underestimate how much sexier you feel wearing a pretty bra. And don't just take my word for it...Lingerie specialists figleaves.com say that more than 70 per cent of women wear the wrong size bra. The most important feature of any bra is the fit, and yet many women go through life wearing the wrong back size, wrong cup size, or both.

FILL YOUR CUPS

★ Bras are sized according to 'band size', which is the measurement around your ribcage immediately under your breasts, and 'cup size', which is the measurement around the fullest part of your bust.
★ Have yourself measured by a professional bra fitter. Most good department stores and Marks and Spencer will have trained assistants who can help you.
★ But remember that sizes vary according to brand and style. So even once you know your correct size, always try a bra on first before buying.
★ It's also worth remembering that your breast size can increase just before a period. If you notice a big difference, it may be worth investing in a bigger cup size for this time of the month.
★ When trying on a bra you should always start on the loosest hook.

A bra can increase by up to four inches through wear and washing.

IT'S THE RIGHT SIZE IF ...

★ The band feels tight but you can still fit two fingers at the back and one at the front.
★ Underwiring is flat against your breastbone at the front and sits on the bones at the sides, not on breast tissue.
★ Your bra is at the same level at the back and front. If it rides up at the back, you need a smaller band size.

IT'S THE WRONG SIZE IF ...

★ The straps dig in. This probably means the band is too loose.
★ Your boobs are bulging over the top or spilling out of the sides. This is not a good look and means you need a bigger cup size.
★ The cups are wrinkling or there is a gap. Try a smaller cup size.

Wearing a correctly fitting sports bra can reduce breast movement by 50 per cent, reducing the stress on ligaments and delaying permanent sagging.

Capsule bra wardrobe

There's no such thing as one bra for all occasions, but how many bras does a girl really need?

1 T-shirt bra – which should be smooth, seam-free and give a good silhouette under the tightest top.
2 Sports bra – to prevent bounce, sagging boobs and even neck and backache.
3 Push-up bra – to give you extra oomph and cleavage when you need it.
4 Sexy bra – worn to be seen.
5 Strapless or multiway – to wear under strapless dresses, spaghetti straps, halternecks and racer-back vests.
6 Basic – pretty enough to make you feel confident, but comfortable enough for everyday, with a good shape and in dark and light colours. Alternatively, a T-shirt bra could double up as a basic bra too.

There is a vast range to choose from in each category. It's up to you to try them on to find your favourites and the ones that fit you best.

BE A SMOOTH OPERATOR

Well-fitting, fresh new underwear gives you a real boost. Regularly go through your underwear drawer and throw out anything that no longer fits properly or that is beginning to look faded, grey or generally worn. Also think about the clothes you're wearing on top and the silhouette you want to create.

Choosing the right shapewear is just as important as picking the right bra if you want to enhance your natural assets, smooth your silhouette and convert bulges into curves.

Shapewear has moved on from Bridget Jones-style 'big pants', and there's now a range of styles according to what area of the body you want to concentrate on.

Stomach – big knickers to smooth the tummy are still the most popular. They look almost like ordinary knickers but have an extra support panel at the front to control the tummy and smooth the waist.

Hips and thighs – these are long leg control briefs with longer legs to smooth the outline of your hips and thighs. There is usually a band which grips the top of the leg to stop the briefs rolling up, and there is often a control panel for the tummy too.

Body – as the name suggests, these cover the whole body, smoothing contours and eliminating lumps and bumps. As they have a built-in bra, these are measured in bra sizes. Perfect for under a dress when you want to create a seamless silhouette.

As well as different styles, there are also different levels of control depending upon what you want.

★ Light control smooths and shapes without decreasing your size.
★ Moderate control contains more elastane but is still comfortable enough to be worn all day.
★ Firm control will minimise areas of your body and can make a very noticeable difference to your shape. But these are not usually comfortable enough to be worn for a whole day.
★ Extra-firm control is the highest level of shapewear available and may contain some boning as well as control panels.

As with all underwear, fit is crucial. Too big and it won't do the job properly. Too small and it will be uncomfortable and you may find you've simply shifted your lumps and bumps.

A BRIEF WORD

With so many styles of knickers to choose from thongs to tangas, shorts to French knickers to briefs, everyone has their favourites. Now, I don't want to impose my choice, but it's worth thinking about what you're wearing on top and the outline that your chosen pair will give you. Also, do you really want that thong on show above the waistband of your jeans when you're tying your child's shoelace in the playground? Or that lacy black pair outlined through your white skirt?

It's all in the fit – remember that a good fit is crucial. Too tight and you'll end up with VPL and unsightly muffin bumps. Too loose … well, let's just say that too much material and wrinkles could be the least of your problems.

Most bras come with matching knickers and I personally think that's the best option for making you feel completely groomed and well put together from the inside out. And I always think you never know what emergencies might arise – at least you'll be able to de-robe with confidence.

PREENING AND CLEANING

It's not only knowing what to put into your closet and what to throw away that's important, you also need to look after what's in there. Just as your hair, face and body need regular maintenance, so do your clothes and shoes. As a general rule I think you should de-clutter your wardrobe and underwear drawers at least twice a year, at the beginning and end of every season. At the same time, it's a good opportunity to make sure your clothes and shoes are in tiptop order.

For example:
★ Dry clean that winter coat.
★ Sew on any missing buttons and make any necessary repairs.
★ Underwear in general, and bras in particular, benefit from regular hand washing, but that's not always practical. A simple solution to help everything last longer is to use a lingerie laundry bag for machine washing on a gentle cycle.
★ Always follow washing instructions carefully, especially for delicate items and woollens. If in any doubt, dry clean.
★ Shoe therapy – take the time to go through your shoes and make a pile ready to take to the cobbler to be re-heeled. They'll last longer and you'll start the season looking groomed.
★ Polish shoes regularly and brush suede to keep them in tiptop condition.
★ Shoetrees help shoes keep their shape and stay looking newer for longer.

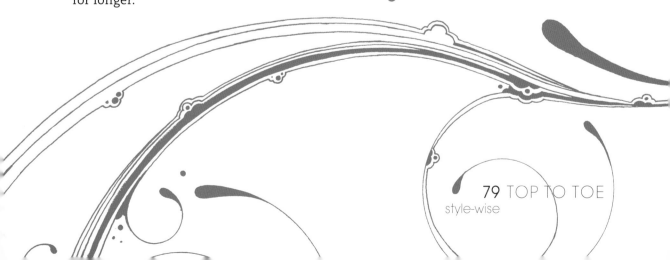

DE-TRAMPED

The foundations are in place. You're groomed, body beautiful, hair and make-up all just so, and with exactly the right underwear to make the most of your assets and, let's not forget, a de-cluttered wardrobe with lots of space to fill. Now what to wear?

This is the fun part, where you get to rebuild your wardrobe and develop your own unique sense of style. Before you head off to the shops, let's take a moment to think about the look you want to achieve.

'LOOKING GOOD AND DRESSING WELL IS A NECESSITY.' **OSCAR WILDE**

VENUS OR VIXEN?

Decide on a signature style. By this I mean something that really works for you and fits with the lifestyle you lead. Vivacious women can't really morph into enigmatic Garbos without ending up cutting a sorry figure. Neither can a quiet woman turn wildcat overnight. But changing the way you dress can bring out your true self and give you more confidence to express your views and rekindle your sense of adventure. Grrrrrr, never say never!

CELEBRITY STYLE ICONS

Celebrities understand just what an impact a recognised signature style can have. Some are so identified with a particular look or item of clothing that they are rarely seen without it. Just think of…

Anna Wintour's bob and sunglasses
Elizabeth Hurley's white jeans
Scarlett Johansson's red lipstick
Victoria Beckham's sunglasses and pout

The most stylish also know when it's time to adapt their look. Sienna Miller moved on from her trademark boho chic and Kate Moss is always ahead in the fashion stakes.

Think about what you do day to day. There's no need for a wardrobe full of sleek business suits if you work from home, or boxes of high heels if you spend most days ferrying kids around – although that's not to say you shouldn't have a few spikes stashed away for when the opportunity arises to strut your stuff.

In order to become one stand-out person you need to adopt a style that you feel comfortable with, but not *so* comfortable that you never make an effort to get out of your fleece. So think hard, who are you really, deep inside, that you want to perfect the art of outside? Are you a woman of mystery? The eternal tomboy? Ms overtly sexy? Ms covertly sexy? A drama queen?

WHAT'S YOUR STYLE?

STYLE PROFILE	Is a bit of a…	Loves	Dislikes
★★★★★★★★★★★★★★★★★★★★★★★★★★★★★★★★★★★★★★			
Mysterious	Muse. Likes to be unpredictable	Surprises	Predictable people who always look the same
★★★★★★★★★★★★★★★★★★★★★★★★★★★★★★★★★★★★★★			
Eternal Tomboy	Lad. Loves to do physical things and get her hands dirty	Wears practical clothes that don't cost the earth	High heels and make-up. Anything awkward and fussy
★★★★★★★★★★★★★★★★★★★★★★★★★★★★★★★★★★★★★★			
Overtly Sexy	Tart – in the nicest sense of the word. Loves to look curvaceous and sexy	Sexy underwear	Shapeless clothes and dull colours
★★★★★★★★★★★★★★★★★★★★★★★★★★★★★★★★★★★★★★			
Covertly Sexy	Tease. A librarian by day and temptress by night	To feel comfortable and look elegant without being overdone	Brash, over-confident women
★★★★★★★★★★★★★★★★★★★★★★★★★★★★★★★★★★★★★★			
Drama Queen	Diva. Loves to be the centre of attention. Is the heart and soul of the party	Chunky jewellery and bright colours	Shy, frumpy women

Never goes anywhere without…	Favourite colours	Style	Celebrity
Her mobile phone	Metallics, aquamarine, purple, teal, scarlet	Eclectic. A close follower of fashion but has a definitive style	Kate Moss
Her jeans	Blues and browns	Masculine and practical. Is a jeans, trainers and T-shirt girl. Nothing fussy or high maintenance	Cameron Diaz
Red lipstick	Black, white, red, shocking pink	Loves to flaunt her assets. Always wears fitted, tailored clothes	Dita Von Teese Marilyn Monroe
Her pearls	Greys, pinks and browns. Soft pastels and earth shades	Loves to look elegant and sophisticated	Catherine Zeta-Jones or Charlotte from Sex and the City
A killer pair of high heels	Yellow, gold, red	Flamboyant. Loves to wear clothes with a stand-out factor. Bold patterns, colours and lots of texture	Donatella Versace

These are just a few examples. You might find you fit into more than one of these profiles or perhaps something entirely different. The beauty is, when it comes to establishing a signature style, you make the rules.

Once you've identified the image you'd like to project, it's infinitely easier to create a sense of style because you know what you're aiming for. Use magazines to help inspire you and focus your mind around the look you want to achieve. You need to approach your new look in the same way you would an interior design project. If you were decorating your bedroom, you would go through lots of magazines to get a feel for the type of style you want, from colours through to furnishings and accessories. This approach also helps you narrow down a list of stores to visit. Creating a new look for yourself requires pretty much the same powers of deduction and creativity.

OWN YOUR STYLE

Now that you've identified your style profile, look outwards and identify others who match your persona. Study them. Learn from them. Very few of us are trendsetters, the majority of us just follow fashion, watching what others do and customising it to suit ourselves. Sometimes, trying too hard to be different makes you stand out for the wrong reasons. You need to wear your new style with flair, and more importantly with consistency. That is how you take ownership of a look until it becomes one with you. In the same way as red and white is synonymous with Coca-Cola, your new identity needs to be an extension of who you are. The only way to achieve this is to be your image until people identify you in just that way. That's when you become more than just a person and you become a brand – someone with a point of difference that sets you apart from those around you. Before you know it, it will become part of your innate make-up too. Don't get me wrong, a few outfits are not enough to cultivate a signature style, it takes a lot of effort and commitment, but it will be worth it – and it's a lot of fun too.

NO BODY'S PERFECT

Once you've established the look you want to go for, you need to make it work for your body shape. Let's face it, nobody's perfect; the secret is knowing how to make the most of what you've got. Remember your TDF factor? If it happens to be your slim waist or your gorgeous legs, now's the time to make the most of them.

Most of us fall into one of five distinct body shapes – apple, pear, rhubarb (rectangular), strawberry (inverted triangle) and hourglass. With a little know-how and confidence we can use clothes to disguise our worst features and, more importantly, enhance our best. Use these simple guidelines to help you identify your body shape and make the most of your assets.

style-wise

IF YOU'RE AN APPLE ...

★ You have a large, voluptuous chest ★ Arms tend to be chunky
★ You carry weight around the tummy ★ Your legs are slim

DO:

★ Wear V-necks or wraparound tops to break up your torso and make the most of your cleavage.

★ Make sure your bra is the correct size and gives you a defined silhouette. For large busts, a minimiser might be an option to help define proportions better.

★ Wear tailored jackets and coats that nip in at the waist, but avoid the double-breasted variety. Single-breasted jackets are more slimming.

★ Choose just one or two colours to slim you down and draw attention away from lumps and bumps. For example, wear a darker colour on top with a brighter shade below to attract attention to your slim pins.

★ Opt for fitted tops that fall just below your belt line.

★ Wear pencil skirts to show off your shapely pins.

★ Choose wide-leg trousers to balance your frame.

★ Choose low-waisted or flat-fronted trousers with a side zip for the most flattering cut.

★ Look for three-quarter length or long, fluted sleeves which are more flattering.

★ Accessorise wearing large, chunky belts around the hips to give the illusion of a waist and draw attention away from a flabby tummy.

DON'T:

★ Wear clingy tops as they tend to ride up to reveal rolls of flab.

★ Choose busy patterns on your top half as they will emphasise any extra inches.

★ Opt for polo necks. They make you look top heavy and as if you have no neck. The idea is to emphasise those sexy curves without adding bulk.

★ Wear narrow straps or cap sleeves if your arms are heavy. They will draw attention to the widest part of your arm.

TRICKS OF THE TRADE:

★ Experiment leaving tailored jackets and coats undone to slim and add definition to your waist. This also helps elongate the body by creating a vertical line which helps slim down proportions.

★ When buying a jacket, always try a smaller size as it often holds its shape better when worn open, which is more flattering. If you prefer to wear your jackets buttoned up, a bigger size may be preferable to avoid pulling around the buttons.

★ Wear a darker colour top and bottom under a fitted jacket in a brighter or lighter shade, as this will conceal all imperfections.

★ Draw attention to your wrists (which usually remain slim even if arms are heavy) by wearing three-quarter-length sleeves and bracelets.

★ Invest in some tummy support underwear such as waist-cinchers or control pants, to give you an added confidence boost when you need it most.

YOUR PERFECT JEANS:

★ To show off your slim pins, opt for straight or very slightly boot-cut legs.

★ Avoid drainpipes at all costs as this will make you look top-heavy, while wide-leg jeans won't show off your legs to their true potential.

★ For extra-slim legs, frosting, shading or embroidery on the denim will add texture and definition.

★ Pocket detailing on the back will help give your bum the shape it needs.

★ To avoid muffin tops, opt for a mid-rise or even a high-rise waist to hold you in place and give you a smoother line.

IF YOU'RE A PEAR ...

★ You probably have beautiful shoulders ★ A small chest ★ Slim arms ★ A tiny waist
★ Curvaceous hips ★ You carry weight on your bum and thighs

DO:

★ Keep attention focused on your upper body.

★ Choose patterned tops or ones with interesting details such as horizontal stripes, gathering, embellishment or bold prints.

★ Wear eye-catching earrings, necklaces or big brooches to draw attention upwards.

★ Try wide slash-neck tops to play up your shoulders and balance the width of your hips.

★ Wear three-quarter-length coats and jackets which skim over your bottom and thighs. Or cropped jackets that are nipped in at the waist. The key is that the jacket should sit either above or below your thighs but not on them.

★ Tailored skirts and dresses are more flattering.

★ A-line skirts skim over wide hips.

★ Wear a dark colour on your lower half.

★ Restrict patterns and bright colours to tops, jackets and coats.

★ Low-rise trousers make bottoms looks smaller.

★ Boot-cut or flared trousers create a more balanced silhouette.

★ Bootleg hipsters avoid the 'gaping waist' problem.

DON'T:

★ Wear short skirts if you've got chunky calves. Opt for trousers instead, as long skirts can be frumpy. If you feel more comfortable in a long skirt, make sure you team it with hip accessories to keep it young and fresh, e.g. hipster belts, chunky beads or boots.

★ Choose bias cut skirts as these cling in all the wrong places, emphasising the width of your hips and thighs.

★ Wear bright colours or eye-catching patterns on your bottom half.

★ Wear trousers with gathered or belted waistbands – they just add volume to your hips.

TRICKS OF THE TRADE:

★ Wear a push-up bra to give your boobs some oomph and balance out your hips. Padded, gel, and air-filled bras will also add volume and definition to your chest.

★ Boots help disguise chunky calves. Most retailers now offer a wide fit for larger calves.

★ Always make sure your skirts cover your knees and the tops of your boots.

★ Wearing heels lengthens and slims legs.

★ Wedges help balance out thick calves.

★ Get your trousers lengthened or shortened to fit. Most dry cleaners offer an alterations service.

★ Pointy-toed shoes help to slim calves by lengthening the leg. Open toes are also flattering as they soften the foot and elongate the leg.

★ Waisted belts help draw attention to your slim waist and create more of an hourglass shape.

YOUR PERFECT JEANS:

★ Low-rise bootlegs will slim down hips, elongate legs and balance out proportions by adding width at the ankle.

★ Avoid wide legs or jeans with heavy pocket detailing front or back.

★ Opt for flat-fronted styles as these are more slimming on the hips.

★ The darker the colour and more stretchy the fabric, the slimmer your curves will appear.

★ Also look for jeans where shading is darker on the hips and lighter at the bottom as this will draw the eye downwards thereby lengthening the leg. Alternatively, opt for jeans where shading is darker on the outside of the leg and lighter on the top of the leg as this will help slim down the thighs.

★ The longer the better, and always wear with heels.

IF YOU'RE A STRAWBERRY...

★ You have a wide back and broad shoulders ★ A full bosom ★ You carry most weight around your tummy ★ Your arms can be heavy

DO:

★ Wear deep V-necks or wide scooped necklines to soften your shoulders.

★ Wraparound tops can also be a good choice as they soften the shoulders.

★ Opt for tailored shirts, but make sure the buttons don't bulge over your cleavage and tummy or all the way down.

★ Choose tailored jackets and coats without belts for the most flattering shape.

★ Opt for knit tops or dresses with a bit of stretch as these will help define your shape more easily. Note: you may need to try a size up to avoid anything too clingy.

★ Layering knit cardigans over tops will help define waist and soften shoulders.

★ Wear hipster belts off-centre to attract attention away from your chest or torso.

★ Emphasise your slim legs with fitted skirts.

★ Choose elegant, high heels with or without an ankle strap to draw attention to your shapely legs.

DON'T:

★ Button coats or jackets up to the neck – this will just add bulk and make you look shapeless.

★ Wear high necks or polo necks as these will create a solid block of colour making you look top heavy.

★ Choose bold patterns for your top half as this will draw attention to your wide shoulders and large chest.

★ Opt for heavy wool sweaters as this adds bulk.

TRICKS OF THE TRADE:

★ Wrap dresses are particularly flattering because they accentuate your waist and soften the bust by creating a more flattering V-neck.

★ A professionally fitted bra is essential as this will lift and separate the bust and make a huge difference to the way clothes look on you.

★ If you're not comfortable with your cleavage, opt for a minimiser bra to help reduce the volume of your chest.

YOUR PERFECT JEANS:

★ Wide leg or boot-cut styles will help balance out your hips and your shoulders.

★ Wear with chunky hipster belts to draw attention away from your waist and add width to your hips, balancing out your shoulders

★ The wider the waistband, the more shape it will give to your bum – as will high pockets on your derrière.

★ Avoid super-low-rise cuts as these will encourage your tummy to bulge over the top.

IF YOU'RE A RHUBARB ...

★ You're probably slim ★ With a boyish, straight up and down figure ★ You have a distinct lack of curves ★ And may have a long body in proportion to your legs – which can be long and lanky too. ★ You have model proportions and are able to carry off strong catwalk looks – if you choose.

DO:

★ Wear high-necked tops, e.g. crew or polo necks. You can also get away with bulkier, more textured knits.

★ Wear layered tops and T-shirts to add bulk and inject shape.

★ Choose fitted or tailored jackets and coats that hug the waist and flare over your hips to give the illusion of a waist.

★ Look out for sleeveless tops to make the most of your slim arms. If your arms are super skinny, capped sleeves will add bulk and shape to the arm.

★ Vest tops and sleeveless jumpers are also great choices, especially layered over shirts.

★ Look for structured clothes, which help to create curves and disguise your lack of boobs or waist. Or add volume with garments that create curves, for example puffball skirts or flared trousers.

★ Pick shorter skirts to show off your legs.

★ If your legs are super skinny, opt for mid-calf-length pencil skirts – the tighter the better – which will also flatter you.

★ Opt for well-fitted slimline trousers to emphasise your height and slender frame.

★ Wear waisted belts to create the illusion of a waist.

DON'T:

★ Wear full or gypsy skirts – they will simply drown you, unless you have the height to pull them off.

★ Choose anything baggy or unfitted if you want to create a sexy curvaceous look, unless you're super skinny, when added volume can help to define curves.

★ Opt for baggy trousers – they'll draw attention to your lack of curves and make you look wider at the same time. Not a winning combination.

TRICKS OF THE TRADE:

★ The key is to break up the body as much as possible, so avoid wearing one colour from top to toe.

★ Add interest and colour with accessories.

★ Emphasise your slim arms and shoulders with sleeveless tops and capped sleeves.

★ Padded, push-up bras can increase chest size and improve proportions.

YOUR PERFECT JEANS:

★ If you're slim and petite, skinny or drainpipe jeans show off your lean figure and slim proportions.

★ To play down your height, go for a pair that stop at your ankle and team with pumps.

★ Wide-leg jeans will add volume to your willowy frame. Team with cropped jackets or nipped-in shirts and waisted belts.

IF YOU HAVE AN HOURGLASS FIGURE ...

★ You are curvaceous ★ You have a full chest ★ A small waist ★ Rounded hips
★ Your legs may tend to be heavier

DO:

★ Wear V-neck tops for a hint of cleavage.
★ Opt for 1950s-style sweetheart necklines that will flatter your boobs and draw attention away from heavy arms.
★ Choose fitted, cropped jackets that nip in at the waist.
★ Capitalise on your curves. You have the ideal body shape so embrace it: don't hide it under your clothes.
★ Invest in a pair of tailored trousers. Well-fitted black ones are ideal to slim your legs.
★ Wear heels to elongate your legs and lift your bottom.

DON'T:

★ Hide your curves under baggy layers.
★ Wear empire waistlines or drop waists, as they will make you appear either top or bottom heavy.

TRICKS OF THE TRADE:

★ Make a point of emphasising your waist.
★ Wear a belt or tailored jacket that's fitted at the waist.
★ Skirts are often more flattering than trousers.
★ Worn with boots, skirts can help disguise heavy legs and create a leaner shape; they create a more uniform, elongated look and enable you to experiment with shorter skirts, which you wouldn't otherwise be able to get away with.
★ Wear plunging necklines to enhance cleavage, or invest in a minimiser bra if shy.

YOUR PERFECT JEANS:

★ Hipster jeans are the most practical as they avoid the fitted-waist versus fitted-on-the-hip dilemma.
★ Boot-cut styles are still the most flattering shape for you. Ignore catwalk trends and opt for something that's guaranteed to make you look slim and sexy.
★ The darker in colour, the more slimming on the leg.
★ Avoid heavy detailing on the pockets or embellishment on the legs as this will only divert attention away from your key asset, which is your waist.

Silky, flimsy material tends to emphasise any bulges. Thicker, stretchy fabrics are usually more flattering and easier to wear.

IN THE MOOD

Whether you're aware of it or not, most of us are mood dressers.
If you're in a good mood you'll wear something bright and cheerful,
and as a result attract compliments which will further boost your
confidence and attract even more positive energy.

   If you're feeling low, you're more likely to wear something safe,
usually dark or dull; this will make you feel worse, not better, and
no one is likely to pay you much attention – which, girls, is what
we all love to get…right?

SHOW YOUR TRUE COLOURS

Colour's a wonderful thing and, whether or not we're aware of it,
our entire existence is governed by the colours around us. Colour can
affect our mood and the colours we choose to wear can define our
personalities. Now, I'm not a big advocate of colour charts, as I think
it's more important to experiment with colour than avoid it for fear
of wearing the wrong thing. However, an understanding of the impact
a colour can have on your mood as well as those around you can be
a powerful tool in your wardrobe.

Neutrals complement a cool, collected persona – a woman who
likes to walk in the park, the touch of rain on her skin; one who isn't
easily thrown. That said, if you're a whiter shade of pale, I wouldn't
recommend a wardrobe of taupe and grey colours for you as this
will only wash you out even more. Go instead for bright whites, crisp
creams or brighter pastels like turquoise and pinks, as these will
inject some life into your skin.

   Red is the colour of danger, sexy Hollywood sirens and warning
signs. No other colour attracts so much attention. If you want to be
seen, wear scarlet. Red is for vamps who know they look good and
aren't scared to flaunt it. But even if you're not well known for your
vamp tendencies, I would most certainly recommend you invest in

a little red number. It can transform the shyest dormouse into the l
ife and soul of the party. One of my friends only ever wore black – she
just didn't feel she had the figure or the confidence to wear anything
else (though I might as well point out that she was a size 8, so heaven
knows what mirror she was using). Anyway, I took her shopping and
found her a killer red dress and heels. It has totally transformed her
life. She now makes a point of never wearing black unless she has
to; she's more confident, feels sexier and is more comfortable in her
skin. So you see the colours you wear really do make a difference and
are often a reflection of how you feel about yourself. So go on, try out
a splash of red next time you hit the town; you'll be amazed at how
good it makes you feel. Vamp to vixen here we come!

Browns and other earth tones are for the quietly sexy woman,
who likes to stay in touch with her roots. Brown is the 'new black'
and is softer and more flattering for most skin tones. It's also a good
complement for many other colours as it is more versatile and
kinder than black, particularly as we get older.

Black can be slimming, but head to toe black absorbs light and
drains your complexion. It implies you are independent and a bit of a
loner but it can also suggest an underlying insecurity and self-doubt.
Remember too that it's the colour we associate with villains. Opting
for black every day can mean you want to blend into the background.
On the other hand, for evenings out, the little black dress – whether
classic, slinky, or bang up to date – is still a hard-to-beat wardrobe
staple. *Just don't wear it all the time, as 'staple' isn't 'sexy'.*

★ Green lowers the heart rate and blood pressure and helps
muscles relax. Red and orange have the opposite effect.
★ We may associate red with anger, but people are more likely
to argue and babies to cry in yellow rooms.
★ If you want to boost your communication skills at work, ditch
the black and opt for turquoise blues instead.

Pinks are worn by the demure dolls, the ones who capitalise on their innate innocence. Pink and other rosy shades can also suggest romance and are very feminine.

Mauves are inherently sensual, and are for the woman who doesn't shy away from her sensuality. Purple was traditionally the colour of royalty, a favourite of Cleopatra's. Today it's often linked with spirituality and the senses. I like to associate purple with passion.

Blue is associated with the imagination and creativity. I know several women who avoid navy because they were forced to wear it as school uniform, but it's a very wearable alternative to black – elegant, slimming and more flattering than black if you're feeling tired or your skin is pale.

Green gives an impression of calm; after all, it's the colour of nature. However, some think green suggests you are an observer who tends to hold back. Editors often avoid putting green on magazine covers because it makes them harder to sell and green cars are renowned for having more accidents than any other colour.

'IF YOU ARE TRYING TO IMPRESS YOUR BOSS IN THE FIRST FEW MONTHS OF WORK, GREEN IS THE COLOUR OF GENUINE COMMITMENT, SHOWING YOUR DEDICATION TO YOUR WORK.' **DIANA MOSSOP**

Is there a colour you love but whenever you wear it you notice your hair looks drab or your face appears drawn? The chances are it's no coincidence. Colours that suit your skin tones and hair colour will instantly lift and brighten your complexion or enhance the colour of your eyes. Be brutal as you assess your clothes. Give the boot to anything that doesn't give you a boost. And if you still love that particular shade, you can still wear it – on belts, bags, shoes or other accessories – just not next to your face.

Experts agree that bright colours generally create an impression of confidence but warn that they will get you noticed. If you wear bright colours to an interview or important meeting you should be prepared to speak out and make sure you know what you're talking about. Red can be a good choice for a meeting if you're keen to get your viewpoint across – though a word of caution: some may regard you as too confrontational.

It seems that the colours you choose may be revealing more about you than you realise. Think about what they actually say about you. Do they represent who you are? Perhaps, most important of all, do they suit you and make you feel better about yourself? Having a wardrobe that always boosts your spirits and hides your insecurities will help you go places faster. As women, we need to capitalise on our female assets as much as possible by ensuring our clothes exude femininity and sexuality (however subtle). This will ensure you're noticed and people pay attention to you, which is only going to make you feel more confident in your own skin.

THE ICING ON THE CAKE

In my book, the one thing that differentiates the stylish from the average is the use of accessories. Fashion trends come and go; some we like, some we don't. To look good you don't have to be fashionable. Yes, it's important to keep an eye on the trends, the cuts, colours and shapes that are in season – but to truly define your own niche you need to become a dab hand at accessorising. By this I'm not just talking about necklaces and earrings. I'm talking about anything that doesn't actually serve the purpose of covering up exposed flesh. Any extras over and above your top and trousers are classed as accessories. I'm talking about your shoes, handbags, necklaces, earrings, bracelets, scarves, belts and even some jackets/capes could be classed as an accessory to your outfit.

Accessories not only give you a more stylish edge, they are an easy, cost-effective way to remain fashionable. Clever use of accessories can also help draw attention away from anything you'd rather hide and towards your TDF factor. Think about it girls, if you've got great legs, your shoes are going to help focus attention on your pins.

I'd go as far as to say that at least one-third of your clothing budget should be spent on accessories. This will enable you to not only look more stylish but get more out of your existing wardrobe, too. Only problem, once you start it can become addictive ... if you could see my belt collection!

SHOP TILL YOU DROP

Right girls, we've talked style, shape and colour, it's now time to put the theory into practice and hit the shops. But hold on a minute – no point rushing out and grabbing anything that fits. A good shopper never leaves the house without a strategic plan of action. First port of call – a capsule wardrobe. I have to say that the word 'capsule' is so far removed from images of style and fashion it's hard to feel inspired. I prefer to think of it as the heart of your wardrobe. The centre from which any number of looks can be created – now that's a more exciting prospect.

WARDROBE ESSENTIALS

The clothes you wear will depend upon the life you lead. Obviously everyone has different needs, and you may already be able to see where the gaps are. But I believe there are ten basic essentials that every woman should have in her wardrobe. These are:

1 Little black dress
2 Classic trench coat
3 Crisp white shirt
4 Luxurious cashmere sweater – wool is a cheaper alternative
5 The 'perfect' jeans – no mean feat
6 Tailored jacket
7 Gorgeous black trousers that make you look slim and sexy no matter what
8 A knee-length skirt
9 A pair of sexy court shoes that can be worn all year round
10 Fabulous leather handbag

You're probably thinking: what about T-shirts, tops, dresses, boots? Remember the capsule is the heart or core of your wardrobe, which you can add to each season to create a new look. The good news is with these ten timeless classics in your wardrobe you will never have a style crisis again. Each item is versatile and can be mixed and matched within the capsule as well as with other items in your wardrobe.

It's always best to think in terms of complete outfits, putting clothes together for daytime as well as evening, along with accessories.

Once you've identified which pieces of the capsule you need to get, the secret is to spend some time and money on the basics. These ten items form the backbone of your wardrobe, so it's worth investing in pieces that will go the distance and make you look expensive. Each season you can easily add trend pieces to your capsule in order to update your look. For instance, you may swap your skinny jeans for high-waisted flares or a shift dress for a wrap dress – but the core pieces stay the same.

It's actually quite liberating to think how few clothes we actually need and how many looks we could create out of ten timeless items, don't you think? This doesn't mean to say you can't have a signature style. Once you've got your capsule in place, use high fashion pieces and accessories to individualise your look. For example, team jeans with a T-shirt, headband and bug-eye specs for weekend cool. Alternatively, mix jeans with white shirt, tailored jacket, chunky necklace and heels for a more stylish feel, or layer cashmere sweater over white shirt and jeans for a more preppy look. The options are endless.

To ensure your capsule wardrobe's as versatile as possible, it probably makes sense to go for more neutral colours for the building blocks and add vibrant pieces to create flair and individuality.

Whether you're a career girl, housewife or sexy singleton – each and every one of us needs to have these ten staple items in our wardrobe. I defy anyone who disagrees to convince me otherwise.

ARMED AND READY FOR ACTION?

You've got the look; you've identified the gaps in your wardrobe and the capsule essentials you have to buy. It's definitely time for some shopping action. Now I'm not suggesting you all have to hire a personal stylist. Most department stores offer a personal shopping service free of charge, but more importantly I want to get the message across to you that image counts. It's so easy when you're young; shopping is a fun, social weekend activity. But for most of us women, juggling families and careers, shopping for ourselves becomes a long-forgotten pastime, a daunting activity that can terrify and destroy the little confidence we have. No more! Here are my five top shopping tips to set you on your way:

1 *Set a budget.*

It's all fine and well embarking on a shopping spree, but a hefty credit card bill's enough to wipe the smile off anyone's face. Set yourself a budget before you go and try to stick to it, give or take a hundred pounds either way. This will ensure you stay focused and don't get distracted by things that aren't essential.

2 *Make a list.*

Be really specific about what you need. Walking into a shop can be overwhelming and often you don't know where to begin. Having a specific list will ensure you don't end up with a cupboard of clothes you don't need.

3 *Only shop for yourself.*

It's very easy to fall into the trap of getting sidetracked and buying things for your partner and kids. This is about you, and developing a signature style that you are comfortable with. It's simply impossible to do this while shopping for your children at the same time.

4 *Make time.*

Going shopping with your kids in tow or between appointments will only end in frustration. Even the best personal shoppers in the world will tell you they can't work miracles in an hour. If you're embarking on developing a new signature style, you need to set aside a morning or an afternoon to give you enough time to make the right decisions. Shopping under pressure only leads to expensive mistakes.

5 *Be prepared.*

Take key wardrobe essentials with you. No point trying to find evening tops to wear with your jeans if you don't have your jeans with you. Similarly, trying on dresses without heels is farcical. The right underwear will also help you visualise the final look more easily.

And finally …

To look good is a lifetime commitment. It's not for a season, only
to be lost and forgotten once the stress of life takes over. You start
small and slowly build a wardrobe you can rely on for every occasion,
which you can subtly adapt and add to over the years as you age and
fashions change.

Looking the part is more than half the battle won. I've worked
with so many women whose outlook on life has completely changed
when they took the time to change their image. You might think this
a superficial pastime, and that may be true, as long as you're happy
with the way you look. If not, you have nothing to lose and so much
to gain by giving your style a boost.

This is the fun bit! This is where you get to design and mould
your true identity. One that evolves with time but never loses that
definitive uniqueness that is quintessentially you, which allows you
to face the world and life's challenges with confidence.

Right, my little glamour-puss, you're looking fantastic, but I know
deep down inside you've always wanted to drop a dress size. Well,
here's how …

CHAPTER FIVE

The proof's in
the pudding

STUCK IN A FAT RUT?

Many of us have tried every diet fad that has ever been published,
joined Weight Watchers, consulted a dietician, and yet are still no
closer to achieving our 'ideal' body shape – one that's fit for a bikini
or even a tankini at a push. Added to that, our self-image is not
helped by the awful lighting and mirrors you find in shop changing
rooms. Is it just me, or do they always make you look as if your
cellulite's magnified overnight? I've succumbed to removing my
glasses on principle when trying on swimwear and clothes, as I find
a little blurring round the edges is a wonderful thing; I call it my
instant airbrush. Being short-sighted can have its advantages – you
may wish to reconsider that laser eye surgery … But the point about
fatness, and thinness, is that it has become an obsession for many
women and for our society generally. An industry has grown up around
that obsession and commonsense attitudes towards food (eat less,
exercise more) have been lost. So let's get the basics straight.

DITCH THE DIET

Let me say it from the start. I'm not into diets and, just to be clear,
this chapter is not about *what* to eat. Magazines and books are falling
from the shelves with the latest 'must-try' diet and I'm not going to
add to them. Why? Because if they worked we wouldn't need them.
And let's not forget that the diet industry is a multimillion-pound
business and it's simply not in their interest for you to lose weight.
Think about it: do you want to line someone's pockets or slim down
your own?

'I NEVER WORRY ABOUT DIETS. THE ONLY CARROTS
THAT INTEREST ME ARE THE NUMBER YOU GET IN
A DIAMOND.' **MAE WEST**

What I'm talking about is *how* to eat; or, in other words, changing
your attitude to food and the way you see food. For example, a piece
of dairy-milk chocolate is *not* sensory heaven through which all your
woes will be forgotten as your teeth sink deeper and deeper into the
creamy promise of paradise. Nope, that piece of chocolate is not your
friend. It's a lazy sod that's going to settle itself just where you don't
need any more padding. The sooner we all wake up and distinguish
the friends from the foes in our fridge, the easier life and losing
weight will be.

You've convinced yourself that one little piece of chocolate won't
do any harm; after all, this is for life – and life without chocolate isn't
worth living. That first bite sends you into orgasmic heaven. For a
split second you feel like a princess, slender and beautiful, the envy
of every woman. But…this state of harmony cannot last forever.

As soon as you step back into the big bad world, reality bites. Your
heart rate speeds up and your head starts to thump as inner voices
shout: 'You disgust me, you have no self-control. What is wrong with
you? You don't deserve to live…no wonder you're such a fat pig.'
Sound familiar? A bit extreme perhaps, but we've all been there.

'ONE SHOULD EAT TO LIVE, NOT LIVE TO EAT.'
BENJAMIN FRANKLIN

So, where do we all go wrong? Losing weight is not about food; in
fact it's about changing the way you feel about yourself internally
and externally. Losing weight is as much a mental thing as it is a
physical thing. The reason people so often struggle to lose weight
is not because they aren't committed or don't try hard enough, it's
because their self-esteem is in pieces. Food is simply an accessory

to the crime, and simply focusing on food when trying to diet will not be enough to sustain long-term weight loss. In fact, I firmly believe that the minute we utter the word 'diet', we all start craving things we probably wouldn't normally eat in the first place – at least I certainly do.

It's hardly surprising that most diets fail when for a start the regime is often impractical and antisocial, not to mention unpalatable. Never mind the fact that as soon as it's over you return to the way you ate before, which – need I state the obvious? – is the reason you decided to diet in the first place.

One of the biggest issues when losing weight is that your clothes feel tight; every time you look in the mirror you see fat and cellulite. Everything seems to be screaming yuck! 'You'll never find a man' or, if you've got one, 'How can he bear to see me naked?' Basically, everywhere you look you receive signals that reaffirm you are disgusting, a complete failure, since you can't even control your weight and might as well give up now. For many people, the fridge is the one and only place they can go to hide and indulge themselves in things that make them feel OK. But try to remember that actually, cellulite is not the end of the world, and that you are most definitely not alone in agonising over it. It can be incredibly difficult, but try to keep it in perspective.

DIETS DON'T WORK

'If dieting worked, there would be a bunch of skinny people walking around,' is the view of an expert – Dr David Katz, obesity researcher at Yale University. Recently, another team of researchers working at the University of California, Los Angeles, examined thirty-one weight-loss studies and concluded that long-term dieting might seem to work at first but it was not a long-term solution. They found that between one- and two-thirds of dieters regained all the weight they had lost. 'People should be quite clear that a diet is a temporary fix,' says Traci Mann, psychologist and leader of the study at UCLA.

the proof's in the pudding

Studies pinpoint a number of key reasons why diets fail:
★ they deprive you of vital nutrients and whole groups of food, which in turn…
★ …lowers your metabolic rate, meaning as soon as you stop dieting and eat more normal amounts you pile back on the pounds
★ diets often don't fit in with normal everyday lives working in offices, or family meals, for instance
★ they are usually temporary and do nothing to address your basic eating habits or health
★ dieting is only half the problem as far as losing weight is concerned; you also need to increase physical activity

WHAT DO I NEED TO BE THIN?

In simple terms you need:
★ Positive self-talk and attitude. Love (or at least like) yourself.
★ A wardrobe that makes you feel fantastic, irrespective of which stage of your weight-loss programme you are at.
★ A regular exercise routine (three times a week is ideal – see chapter 6 on page 130).
★ A few good mental strategies for demon-busting – in diet terms this is all about taking the emotion out of eating (see page 121).
★ To follow a healthy eating programme for life. My Slim plan on page 124 will set you in the right direction.

YOU'RE GORGEOUS

One of the solutions to feeling slim is to feel happy with yourself. By that I mean happy with your body exactly as it is *now*.

'You've got to be kidding?' I can hear you say. But I'm perfectly serious. Take a step back and look at yourself in the mirror. Say out loud, 'I have the most beautiful, sexy body. My body is perfect.' I know this is difficult, but even size eights have issues, and don't get me started on size zeros – double, triple or otherwise.

What I am trying to say is that, before you can even think about changing the way you look, you have to feel good about the way you are now.

'TO LOVE ONESELF IS THE BEGINNING OF A LIFELONG ROMANCE.' **OSCAR WILDE**

CURVES TO KILL FOR

Despite the current vogue for skinny celebrities, many buck the trend. Elizabeth Taylor and Marilyn Monroe, two of the most iconic women of the last century, were hardly thin and are still considered both beautiful and sexy.

More recently, rising Hollywood stars like Scarlett Johansson and Jennifer Lopez are celebrated for their curves. The supermodel Jodie Kidd, famous as a teenager for her skinny, waiflike looks, now as an adult has a far more womanly figure, looking healthier, happier and more attractive, presenting herself with new-found confidence and strength.

'I'D MUCH RATHER BE KNOWN AS CURVY KATE THAN AS SOME SKINNY STICK.' **KATE WINSLETT**

A recent *Grazia* magazine survey to find the best beach bodies hid faces so that readers would not be influenced by the celebrities' identities. Coleen McLoughlin, Charlotte Church and Tyra Banks all featured in the top eight, while skinnier actresses such as Keira Knightley and Mischa Barton were not in the running. It seems that people most admire healthy, toned bodies with soft curves.

Tyra Banks speaks out
Supermodel Tyra Banks has always been proud of her voluptuous body. When unflattering photos appeared of her in a swimsuit and the tabloid press mocked her for having put on weight, she was –

not surprisingly – upset. But instead of keeping quiet and waiting for the stories to die down she decided to speak out.

'I've felt pressure to diet but it wasn't for me. Young girls say, "I look up to you, you're not as skinny as everyone else." They feel more beautiful because I'm curvy, and it's OK.' She also decided to appear on her next TV show wearing a skintight red leotard so that viewers could judge her shape for themselves, launching her 'So What?' campaign. Her aim? To encourage women everywhere to say to themselves, 'I'm not perfect – so what?'

And men's magazines tell the same story. A quick glance at FHM's list of the 100 sexiest women in the world includes just as many curvy women: Jessica Alba, Scarlett Johansson, Salma Hayek, Kelly Brook, Rachel Stevens and Beyoncé Knowles are regularly named in the top 20.

Do you still need convincing that curves are in?

Of course there's a difference between curvy and overweight. Try to remember that weight is not just about perceptions of attractiveness; it is also (and much more importantly) about health. If you concentrate on looking well rather than looking skinny you will have taken an important step towards a healthier attitude to your body and the food you eat.

GLAD RAGS
Indulging in some retail therapy is a tried-and-tested approach.

'SHOPPING IS BETTER THAN SEX. IF YOU'RE NOT SATISFIED AFTER SHOPPING YOU CAN MAKE AN EXCHANGE FOR SOMETHING YOU REALLY LIKE.'
ADRIENNE GUSOFF

Stop putting life on hold until you have reached your so-called ideal state of slimness (which I assure you doesn't exist in reality). What people tend to forget is that they can spend a lifetime trying to reach their 'ideal' weight, which in most cases never happens. This means in actual fact they spend a lifetime feeling miserable and not looking their best, when in reality, just because you're not a size twelve yet doesn't mean you can't look attractive. Losing weight takes time; to achieve success it helps to be able to make the most of yourself throughout the process, whatever size you are.

Here are ten things you can do to boost your self-esteem whilst shedding the pounds:

1 *Colour in your hair.* If you are a brunette, a red rinse can put the shine and life back into your hair. If you are blonde, a brush of fine hair glitter can transform your look for an evening out.

2 *Treat yourself to a new handbag.* Most people have one, maybe two functional handbags for everyday use. One in black and one in brown. Why not treat yourself to a small, feminine handbag in your favourite colour? It may not be the most practical purchase, and you won't use it everyday, but when you do, you will love it and it will make you feel great.

3 *Be bold, and wear false eyelashes.* I went to a party the other day and I bought myself some false lashes for £3.50. Well, I felt like a princess all evening, eagerly batting my eyelids as I made conversation. I was so enthralled by my new look, as was everyone else, I didn't have time to think about anything else.

4 *You too can have a Hollywood pout.* Invest in some gloss for your lips. Lip gloss is perennially popular, whether it's worn over lipstick or on its own, it will give your face a fresh lift and leave you feeling fantastic.

5 *Get your eyebrows shaped.* From as little as £10 you can get your eyebrows professionally shaped, which will give your face a lift and make you feel like a superstar. You won't be able to stop looking at yourself in the mirror.

6 *Treat yourself to a new set of underwear.* But don't buy something functional and practical; instead get something that you have always desired but never bought. For example, a matching bra and knickers set in red or pink – whatever takes your fancy. If you feel feminine and sexy, chances are other people will pick up on it too.

7 *Be a bronzed babe.* It's amazing how good an application of self-tan can make you feel. If you worry about streaks, there are also some fantastic bronzing powders on the market that you simply brush on for a little sparkle during the day or an evening out. Don't just save fake tan for the summer months: adding a sheen to pasty-white winter skin will make you look a stone lighter instantly.

8 *Nail it.* Nothing will make you feel as groomed as manicured fingers and toes. It's not often I get time to treat myself to a professional manicure and pedicure but, when I do, I feel like a goddess. I find I'm much more animated when I speak as I wave my hands around frantically trying to show off my perfect tips.

9 *New heights.* When we're carrying around a few extra pounds, it can make us feel short and dumpy. Buy yourself a killer pair of heels in a standout colour or fabric and let your feet do the talking. Not only will they make you look taller and slimmer, they will give you back some all-important girl power.

10 *Tighten up.* This may sound crazy, but tights never make you feel slim and sexy. They always dig in and leave a horrid red line around your stomach and add an inch onto your waistline – not ideal when you're trying to shed the pounds. Why not swap the tights for a sexy pair of suspenders or hold-ups? So what if you don't have perfect thighs, they come in all sizes and are bound to put a naughty smile on your face when sitting in the boardroom or picking the kids up from school. Come on – give it a go, you've got nothing to lose.

Successful weight loss is all about being able to feel good about yourself throughout the journey without relying on food to be your crutch.

'WHEN WOMEN ARE DEPRESSED, THEY EAT OR GO SHOPPING. MEN INVADE ANOTHER COUNTRY.'
ELAYNE BOOSLER

NUMBER-CRUNCHING

We're all obsessed with numbers, from our bank balance, to our weight, to our age and the size of our clothes. The truth is, no matter where we look, it's never the number we hoped for. Our bank balance is usually too low and our weight is usually too high! Stop!

So what if you haven't lost all the weight you'd hoped for – instead of stressing about it, make it work for you. You can still feel gorgeous, whatever size you are. What you really need to lose are your baggy jumpers and start dressing slim. I know you're thinking, 'There's no point in spending money on clothes until I've lost some weight.' Right? Wrong! Let me be a little more specific. I am not saying you should rush out and spend a fortune on clothes for 'oversized' people, as then you would be mentally resigning yourself to your current size. However, spending time to make yourself look fantastic will not only reduce your negative body image but also make you look and feel fantastic now.

the proof's in the pudding

My top tips for dressing slim:

1 Make sure the detail is on the slimmest part of your body. Whether it's texture, pattern, embellishment or the use of accessories.

2 Always make sure you wear fitted clothes on the largest part of your body. Our instinct is to cover up under loose, baggy clothing – but this only serves to make us look bigger.

3 Use accessories to divert attention away from your worst bits towards your best features. For example, if you're pear-shaped, avoid big hipster belts and draw attention to the top half of your body with chunky necklaces or tops with lots of detail. Slim scarves can also help draw the eye down the centre of the body, which elongates the figure to create a slimmer silhouette.

4 Whatever your body shape, always try to create a waist. Even if you carry extra weight around your tummy area, doing this will give you a more curvaceous figure and avoid you looking like a solid block. This is easily done by wearing fitted jackets, fitted tops or belts.

5 Wearing well-tailored clothes will sculpt your body into shape. I believe that the bigger you are the more tailoring you need to invest in. That doesn't mean you have to wear a suit every day; by tailoring I mean clothes that give you shape as opposed to loose, floating items that simply follow your outline.

6 Wear darker colours on the biggest part of your body. I don't mean you only have to wear black. Anything darker works – for example, grey, brown, navy blue, emerald green. The darker the colour, the more light it absorbs and the slimmer you will appear.

7 Necklines can also make a huge difference. V-necks are fantastic for large breasts as they break up the chest area and help draw the

eye down the centre of the body. Avoid high necklines if you're big busted. Pear- and rhubarb-shaped figures can wear most necklines.

8 Thicker, stretchy fabrics are more slimming than soft silky or satin fabrics, as they tend to mould your body into shape, rather than following any bulges.

9 Remember having curves doesn't equal fat. A curvaceous figure is feminine and sexy and what we should all be striving for. So stop wearing shapeless clothes that make you look square and boxy and start flaunting your curves! You will feel slimmer in an instant.

10 Wearing the same colour or tone of colour top and bottom will make you appear taller and slimmer.

11 A bold pattern can be slimming if evenly distributed over an outfit as it confuses the eye. Bold patterns are usually more slimming on a dress than on separates like a top or trousers.

12 Sew up pockets on jackets and trousers to prevent bulging, which simply adds weight and draws attention to where you need it least.

13 Layering a fitted top underneath a floaty kaftan or cardigan will give you a slimmer proportion. Layering is a fantastic tool for hiding imperfections without opting for big and baggy.

14 Don't forget your heels. A few inches can do wonders for your shape, making you look taller and slimmer. Don't go anywhere without them – they will make you feel sexy and enable you to strut with confidence.

15 Oh, and where possible, opt for pointy shoes, as this will help elongate your legs, slimming down proportions.

the proof's in the pudding

HAPPY IN YOUR OWN SKIN

Clothes are a quick, easy solution to boosting self-esteem in the short-term. And, you will find that if you feel sexy and gorgeous in your clothes, you will come across as radiant and confident. Everyone will want what you've got! Which is? Feeling at ease and confident in your own skin, loving and living every moment of your life to the full, not because you've reached your target weight, but because you are happy with being *you*.

'IT MIGHT SOUND A CLICHÉ, BUT BEAUTY FOR ME REALLY DOES START ON THE INSIDE. IT'S LIKE A STATE OF MIND, A STATE OF LOVE IF YOU WILL. THEN, WHATEVER YOU CAN DO ON THE OUTSIDE IS ALL LIKE A BONUS.' **QUEEN LATIFAH**

COUCH POTATO?

In my experience, most people who are conscious of their weight tend to wear clothes that are at least a size too big for them. It's almost as if there's a fear that they won't fit into a smaller size, which is depressing, so they don't even try. Not only that, what you wear can play a large part in how much you eat.

Big and baggy gives us a licence to fill, whereas fitted equals full.
Think about it: when you're feeling blue and decide to have a night in and treat yourself to your favourite things, what's the first thing you'll do? Put on your comfort clothes, which usually include an oversized baggy jumper (probably your husband's, brother's, or – worse still – your ex's), along with tracksuit bottoms or PJs. You then settle yourself on the couch and merrily stuff your face.

Now imagine coming home from work. You've stocked up on your favourite treats, but instead you change into your killer pair of jeans and a gorgeous top (comfy but cool). You start to indulge, only to find that less than halfway through, you're stuffed. Your waistline simply won't expand any further, so you give up, happily sated but not saturated. Next time you're in the mood for a binge, think about what you wear and you might find wearing a corset (you get the picture) or a waisted belt an easy solution to cutting down the calories without cutting out the fun.

SIZE MATTERS

'I EAT MERELY TO PUT FOOD OUT OF MY MIND.'
N.F. SIMPSON

What if I said that each and every one of you has the potential to be thin? What if I told you that the secret is not in a diet, it's in your head? Achieving your goal weight is probably about 70 per cent mental and 30 per cent physical. By this I mean, if you can change the way you think about food, you will find it so much easier to change the way you eat. One of the reasons that diets don't work is that you never see them as a long-term solution; they're always a short-term fix. This means you are forever at their mercy, as you get trapped in the 'sink or slim' cycle.

As I've already said, I've never been one for dieting, but I used to weight cycle between seasons. In the summer I was always slim and in the winter I put on a few pounds. Enough to make my clothes loose in the summer and tight in the winter, so nothing ever quite fitted. Then one day a boyfriend broke up with me because I wasn't sporty enough – as if?! And he also commented that I wasn't slim enough (hello?) – at which point something snapped.

I decided from that moment on that I would break this cycle once and for all. I joined the gym, started weight training and have never looked back. I've been the same size for ten years now, and I have to say there's nothing better than being able to wear everything in your wardrobe – rain or shine. Now my weight never fluctuates by more than a pound either way and as soon as my clothes feel a bit tight I increase my exercise output, so I always feel in control of it.

FOOD FOR THOUGHT

Another reason why most of us struggle to manage our weight is because we are emotional eaters. By this I mean we don't eat to live, we live to eat. Whether we're bored, depressed, happy or stressed, we use our emotions as an excuse to eat. Most of us don't even realise how much we actually consume over a day, as we eat without even thinking about it. If you ask someone what they eat, the answer will usually be, 'I really don't eat much.' Which basically means, 'I don't tend to have three big meals a day, I just have one meal and snack constantly,' so there's no break between eating.

The secret to staying slim is to take the emotion out of eating. I'm not saying you can no longer enjoy food – on the contrary, you should enjoy it even more. What I'm suggesting is that you eat because you're hungry, not because you're bored, depressed or sad. The majority of people aim to eat healthily and in reality they do, but it's the comfort eating in between meals that destroys any good intentions you may have.

Comfort eating is your biggest demon – it's your self-destruct button. If you're able to stop yourself from comfort eating, half the battle is won.

Call me controversial, but I have yet to meet anyone who gained weight by osmosis. Yes, some people are naturally slimmer, while others may have to try harder, but I can guarantee you, no person you think is naturally slim is able to feast on junk food day in day out indefinitely. People may say they're able to eat what they want, but in fact they choose not to.

MIND GAMES

When I practised as a dietician, I spent most of my time helping people lose weight by trying to make them think differently about food. What I found was that, in reality, although someone would come to me crying saying they desperately wanted to lose weight, in actual fact their weight was a useful cushion for all their problems.

They were victims. They thought they wanted to lose weight – but in reality they didn't want it badly enough. They wanted to drop a dress size without trying to change the way they ate, increasing their activity output, or changing their lifestyle for the long term. Why would you go to all that effort when you could down a few cans of Slim·Fast and drop a few pounds instantly?

Why? Because if you really want to change your body shape, it will take time: there is no such thing as a quick fix. We spend hours, days, months and years stuffing our faces with calories and yet, when it comes to shifting weight, we expect a miracle overnight. Putting on weight may seem easy but it takes the same level of commitment as losing it. The only difference is that one requires a little more physical energy than the other, but the mental energy is in essence the same.

The fact of the matter is that if you want a toned, fit body, there is no magic formula – you need to exercise. And once you start exercising regularly you'll discover there are so many benefits to your health and the way you feel, that losing weight becomes almost a side issue. (See Chapter 6 on page 130 for more.)

NICKY'S CHALLENGE

Let me ask you this. How much do you really, really want to be thin? Think carefully about your answer.

What changes and sacrifices are you prepared to make for the rest of your life? Yes, the rest of your life! Being thin is not a birthright; it takes hours of hard work and commitment to maintain. But I promise you the rewards are worth every single drop of sweat. And just imagine, no more health warnings – you will feel and look fitter than you've ever been in your life.

It's time you got out of the fat rut you're in and did something about it. Before you shake your head, think about how good you'll feel when you're pounds lighter. Imagine the weight falling off your shoulders. You know you want to – and here's how.

You have to approach losing weight like a project. Whether you're changing your job or changing your shape, both require the same level of passion and commitment if you're to succeed. And you can. The only thing that's holding you back is your attitude, not your waistline.

the proof's in the pudding

Ten steps to make you thin

If you really think you've got what it takes to be slim, this is what you need to do:

1 *Get out of your comfort zone*. Stop viewing food as a source of happiness and comfort. Food is there to nourish our bodies and keep us fit and healthy. If you're looking for entertainment, take up a hobby or do some exercise. The more interesting your life, the less likely you are to rely on food as a crutch.

2 *Short-term heaven or long-term hell?* When you walk past a bakery and the delicious smell beckons you in – stop and think to yourself, 'If I carry on walking, within five minutes I will have forgotten all about it.' If your mind is trying to coax you in, think, 'I could treat myself to a piece of cake, but do I really want it?' I always say to myself, five minutes to eat and five hours to lose. This sounds like more effort than it's worth – so before I know it I've moved on. Make your mind work for you. Instead of going into a guilt trip about whether or not you should eat the cake, think about it rationally and weigh up the short-term satisfaction versus the long-term distress. Easier said than done, but if you think that a piece of chocolate takes thirty minutes of power-walking to burn off, it might make you think twice.

3 *Less is more*. Often we eat more than we need. Our eyes are bigger than our stomachs, and all we need is a little moderation and control. One of the easiest ways to help yourself is to put less food on your plate or swap to smaller-sized plates. If you're still hungry afterwards, have some more, but this way you won't be eating simply because the food's already there. It will force you to evaluate whether you really need that second helping.

4 *Time to eat*. One of the things I remember most from my days as a dietician is that so many people who were overweight would sit

in front of me, not understanding why they were overweight because they only ate one meal a day, usually at night. Well there's the answer. If this sounds familiar, you are not eating enough, nor at the right time. By this I mean when you're most active. Eating a huge meal at night is the worst thing you can do to your metabolic rate. You need to eat 70 per cent of your calories before 5 p.m. I'm not saying you can't ever go out at night to eat dinner, but 90 per cent of the time you should eat most of your calories during the day.

5 *Big up breakfast.* I know you've heard it all before, but statistics prove that people who eat breakfast are slimmer than people who don't. In fact, I'll even go so far as to say that 90 per cent of the people I've met professionally and personally who struggle with their weight do not eat breakfast. Astounding but true. Why? Because they don't feel hungry in the morning. Why? Because they ate too much dinner last night and went to sleep on a full stomach. Missing breakfast is an easy habit to fall into, and one that will have a huge impact on your weight gain in the long term.

The minute you open your eyes in the morning, think food! That should put a smile on your face – a legitimate excuse to eat: hooray! Preferably choose something high in fibre and nutritious, as this will mean you're less likely to snack before lunch. Even if you don't feel hungry, force yourself to eat something and soon you won't be able to leave the house without breakfast.

'ALL HAPPINESS DEPENDS ON A LEISURELY BREAKFAST' JOHN GUNTHER

'A Nielsen's National Eating Trends survey found that women who regularly ate breakfast cereal weighed around half a stone less than those who rarely did. Eating breakfast has also been shown to help maintain weight loss and is linked to better levels of concentration.' Told you so!

6 *Weight-less.* Throw away the scales. You need to feel thin; you don't need to be told. Numbers are meaningless; let your clothes be a more accurate judge. I guarantee if you found two women who were both a size 8 their weight could differ by as much as a stone. Which means it's all a load of hogwash. You know when your trousers are tight – you don't need scales to tell you. I make a point of never weighing myself, what's the point? We spend our lives being dictated to and told off; I don't need it in my own bathroom. So do yourself a huge favour and get rid of your scales once and for all and let your figure do the talking from now on.

7 *Dump dessert.* Don't buy it! Those extra 'empty' calories at the end of a meal are the ones that can make the difference between lithe and large. Try shopping online: it's far less tempting and you'll end up with what you need, not what you crave (although, if my home delivery is anything to go by, half of it is usually missing).

We all have our ups and our downs. It's when we're feeling low that we reach for the chocolate, crisps and biscuits to make us feel better. If you don't have them to hand, the chances are you won't go out and buy them, as you'll already be in your PJs and slippers by this stage, so getting dressed again will be too much hassle. If you really want a snack – then have one – but try to keep it under control.

8 *Eat because you have to, not because you want to.* Hunger is underrated. Most of us never give our bodies the chance to really feel hungry. We're so busy snacking all day we never experience real hunger – the roar that rises out of the pit of your stomach. If your metabolism is functioning at its optimum, your body will tell you when it needs its next food fix. If you're constantly eating, you don't give your body a chance to efficiently utilise the energy you're feeding it. Give it a try; I challenge you not to eat anything until you feel really hungry. When you do, sit down and eat properly – try not to snack uncontrollably.

9 *Hide and seek.* Look for hidden calories. We all develop habits that may be a fraction of the calories we eat every day, but they add up – and the question is why? Do we need them at all? I got into the habit of eating a Ferrero Rocher chocolate after dinner every night. Now, I know it's not much, but seven a week, thirty-one a month, and it starts to add up. So I decided to stop and was amazed to see I lost a few pounds just by doing that. I'm not suggesting you can't treat yourself now and then, just be aware of when and what you're eating.

By swapping your daily can of Coke for a glass of water you will lose nine pounds a year. Look at the detail and you'll quickly find opportunities to cut out calories you won't even miss. Perhaps you have a packet of crisps with your sandwich every day? Do you really need it? Will you even miss it? Do you actually enjoy it?

You'll find this far less taxing psychologically, as you're not depriving yourself in the way a diet would; you're simply intellectualising about which foods you need and which you could really live without.

10 *For life.* Remember, being slim is a lifetime occupation. You need to consider what you put into your mouth each and every day of your life, for the rest of your life. This may sound daunting, but do a mental check next time someone offers you that slice of cake. Do you really want it? Are you even hungry? The good news is, the healthier your diet, the less junk food you'll crave, so keeping on the straight and narrow becomes a whole lot easier.

the proof's in the pudding

CHAPTER SIX

'EXERCISE: YOU DON'T HAVE TIME NOT TO.' ANON

LOSING WEIGHT IS A WALK IN THE PARK

I can hear the bedsprings groan as you shift uncomfortably, wondering whether you really want to read on. Let me tell you – yes you do, because you are going to look gorgeous. You are going to live the dream and become the woman you have always wanted to be. We've got you out of your fat rut – and you're thinking differently about food. Now we've got to get those feet moving so you can accelerate your way to the slimmer, more gorgeous you.

If you seriously want that hot bod, you've got to do more than think about it. Starving for a week isn't going to work either. Nope, the only way you're ever going to achieve anything close to Cameron Diaz perfection is by getting your butt off the couch and into the open. Not only that, but taking regular exercise is the only way you will ever be really fit for life.

FIVE-MINUTE CHALLENGE

Just do something – anything! Yes, right now. Stop reading this very second and run up and down the stairs five times or hop around the room on one leg. If you're on the tube, get off at the next stop and run to the front or back of the train, whichever is furthest. Whatever 'springs' to mind – just do it. Go on, no one's watching…I dare you!

Welcome back. Wasn't that exhilarating? Got your heart thumping and the blood pumping in your veins? Good for you. Welcome to your exercise programme. You're no longer thinking about it, you've already begun.

EXORCISE THOSE DEMONS

So now you're all on board, what took you so long? Bad weather? Children? Working too hard? Been sick? Injured? The list is endless. We are all masters of our own downfall. For every positive thought we have about exercising, we'll have twenty excuses why not to. Hey, tomorrow's another day, but there simply is no time like the present.

'IF WE COULD GIVE EVERY INDIVIDUAL THE RIGHT
AMOUNT OF NOURISHMENT AND EXERCISE, NOT TOO
LITTLE AND NOT TOO MUCH, WE WOULD HAVE FOUND
THE SAFEST WAY TO HEALTH.' **HIPPOCRATES**

FIT FOR LIFE

Are you still asking the question, why bother? Let me give you my
six good reasons why exercising is a worthwhile thing to do and
then you decide which side of the fence you're going to sit on.

1 *Sanity check*
The beauty of exercising is that it's all-consuming. It's one of those
precious times in your life when you get to do something just for
you. Not for your partner, not for your children, not for your boss
or even a friend – just you. For all the effort you put in, you and only
you will reap 100 per cent of the reward. There are very few things
we do in life for which this holds true. This is your opportunity to
be completely selfish and, at the same time, give yourself some
much-needed mental space to clear the clutter and be creative.
I get some of my best ideas when I'm running round the common.
No one can contact me, there are no emails to respond to – just time
to think about everything or nothing. I find exercising particularly
effective after a frustrating day in the office when I feel like I might
throttle someone.

Regular exercise, if nothing else, will help to keep you sane and
to keep life in perspective. It lifts your mood by releasing feel-good
endorphins into your system, and helps to counter depression.
You'll also find you sleep better and feel less stressed.

Celebrity control

When Cameron Diaz, Drew Barrymore and Reese Witherspoon found themselves facing the very public break-ups of their long-term relationships, they didn't wallow in self-pity. Instead they each decided to take control of their bodies. Self-imposed fitness regimes with extra exercise, including workouts at the gym, swimming and jogging, resulted in all three of them looking sleek, toned and healthy. Magazines and newspapers were filled with pictures of them looking more stunning than ever at red carpet and other events. The stories were all about how fantastic they looked, not about their partners.

'I DO A LOT OF EXERCISE . . . IT KEEPS ME BALANCED AND SANE!' **KIMBERLY STEWART**

2 *The slim factor*

Not many people out there who are a size 8 or 10 will tell you that it comes naturally. Most of us have to work at it day in and day out.

I've never been naturally slim. For as long as I can remember I've exercised at least three times a week. I always felt envious of friends who did very little but were naturally slim. Twenty years later and the tables have turned. Looking slim-tastic is a lifetime commitment. Even slim people have so-called 'fat days' – but instead of eating their way out of them, they'll choose to work out instead.

Here's my theory: it's all about balance.

Put simply, if you don't overspend on your shopping spree, you'll end up with money to spare. On the other hand, if you blow your budget, you'll probably end up broke. In the same way, if your weekly calorie intake is less than your expenditure you'll lose weight. If it exceeds it, you'll gain weight.

Therefore, to lose weight, your output (exercise) has to exceed your input (the food you eat). It's not rocket science, but it's amazing how many people still haven't grasped this simple theory and still think that a miracle diet is out there. Well, I hate to be the one to break it to you, but it's really not. The secret is exercise.

Next time your clothes are feeling a little too close for comfort, remember this. If you want to lose weight you need to exercise at least three or four times a week. If, on the other hand, you're just looking to maintain your weight and fitness, then one or two times a week will keep you on the straight and narrow.

Sarah's story

Let me introduce Sarah. She had spent most of her adult life looking more hippo than hypnotic, till one day she was sitting on the couch watching the start of the London Marathon, when she announced to her family that she would like to attempt to run it. This, let me tell you, is no mean feat for someone who is size 12, never mind Sarah's size 24. She started training that day and ran fifty metres to begin with (not much further than running around your room a few times). She increased this distance daily until, after three years of training and commitment, she finally ran the London Marathon, having lost almost eight stone. This was an unbelievable achievement, particularly for someone of her age (she was fifty-five at the time). It just proves that you can lose weight no matter how large or how old you are. Sarah had tried numerous crash diets over the years and nothing ever worked. Her miracle cure – exercise! Where did she find it? Within herself.

I am always in awe of people who take action and change their lives in whatever shape or form.

Still not convinced? Perhaps Tom's story will persuade you.

Tom's story

For thirteen years, Tom Armour weighed between twenty-six and thirty stone. At one stage his neck measured as much as Victoria Beckham's waist – twenty-three inches, in case you're wondering.

He used to be an enthusiastic and fit rugby player, running and hill climbing in his spare time. He charts his weight gain to not having the time to exercise while building a career as a banker in his twenties. Now forty-five, he's lost almost fourteen stone in just eighteen months and is exercising regularly again. After losing three stone through dieting, Tom joined a gym which, as he still weighed twenty-five stone, took a huge amount of courage.

Now he goes to the gym two or three times a week with his daughters, working out for up to an hour. He walks to the station each day and always climbs the stairs to his eighth-floor office. On holiday, where once he hid indoors, he now swims and dives. Clients who haven't seen him for a few months fail to recognise him.

I know there are other factors, like your metabolic rate and age, which will impact the speed at which you gain or lose weight, but in essence, if you want to lose weight successfully, you have to up your exercise output. Not only will regular exercise help you shed the pounds, it will also tone up your muscles, which no amount of dieting can do – so if you want a pert bottom it's the only way to go.

The good news is the fat-burning benefits of exercise will continue for a good few hours after you're done. Even if you are lying prostrate on the floor, you're still burning fat. It's all good for you, trust me. Think of Sarah – that could be you!

How often?

A stop-start approach to exercise is not effective and may even lead to injury. Start slowly and build up, especially if you're a beginner. The ideal is to incorporate exercise into your normal routine so that it isn't a huge effort.

Recent research from US exercise guru Dr Kenneth Cooper suggests gentle regular exercise is most effective for the body. Strenuous workouts lasting longer than an hour increase free radical damage and age the body and skin.

stuck in the mud?

3 *Sex appeal*

It's no surprise that the way you feel about your body is closely linked to your libido. By this I'm not suggesting that you have to be thin to feel sexy. Quite the contrary, but you do have to feel confident and proud of the way you look – with or without your clothes.

Working out can go a long way towards improving muscle tone, which will help convert flab into fabulous curves. Not only that, by exercising regularly your appetite and stamina for some hanky-panky with your partner will improve dramatically. Hormone levels are boosted, which raise your libido and improve orgasms.

You're also going to need a little cardio fitness to cope with all that heavy breathing: can't have you passing out halfway through. Then there's muscle strength for those positions where you're required to use muscles you probably forgot you had. (Yes, I'm talking about you.) Oh, and let's not forget about flexibility – even the Kama Sutra is achievable if you stretch not just your imagination but your body a little bit too.

Exercise will not only make you feel sexy but could also enhance your bedroom skills – which, let's face it, can always be improved for everybody …

4 *Be a survivor*

What's the first thing that pops into your mind when you think of the elderly? To me it's a walking stick, and a shuffle, as opposed to a stride. Even if that seems a long way away now, life catches up with you pretty quickly.

Regular exercise will go a long way to maintaining a youthful, healthy body that will keep you fit and agile well into old age. We all have dreams of retiring one day and travelling the world with our new-found freedom. And while it's true we have no control over what fate has in store for us, we can control how fit we are and how energetic we feel when we get there. I don't know about you, but the idea of trekking through the Himalayas sounds far more appealing than an organised bus trip for wrinklies.

What's more, we're all having children when we're older, which means if we really want to enjoy our grandchildren we need to maintain our energy levels for a lot longer. This is even before mentioning that regular exercise lowers our risk of developing cancer, stroke, diabetes, heart disease, as well as many other life-threatening illnesses, lowering blood pressure, maintaining bone density and boosting the immune system. So, all in all, if you want to live a long and healthy life, you've got to give your body the best chance – by putting a little effort in to exercise more regularly than you're doing now.

Liz's story

Liz looked fit and slim. She walked every day and looked young for her age, but despite appearances she felt far from fine. She'd suffered with back problems since childhood, which were getting worse as she got older. Despite trying a number of therapies, nothing helped … until a doctor suggested she try Pilates. She was sceptical but gave it a go. Now, four years later, at forty, she's more supple and agile than she's ever been and she can do things that used to be impossible. 'If I go for a week without a workout, I can feel my back stiffening. The benefits are incredible and I only wish I'd tried it years ago.'

I can also vouch for this. I started doing Pilates a couple of years ago as my posture was getting worse and I couldn't sit at my desk for longer than an hour at a time without my back aching. It took a year of hard work but my posture has improved dramatically and back pain is a thing of the past. Regular exercise can give you more energy and a zest for life.

5 Keep smiling

If all this talk of losing weight and changing your life makes you feel overwhelmed and blue – the best thing for you is a little exercise. As I explained before, exercise helps to clear the clutter and enables you to think straight. This in turn will help you to feel more in control of your destiny and the choices you make.

Exercise helps fight depression by stimulating neurotransmitters in the brain that give you that 'feeeel gooood' factor that James Brown was always singing about. Just thirty minutes of exercise, from a brisk walk to a jog round the park, is all you need to stimulate the release of endorphins – and it's completely legal. Just think what you've been missing out on. All those yummy feel-good hormones rushing around your body, filling you with vitality you never knew you had.

And did I mention it's also free? All you have to do is…something. Each and every one of those endorphins has been specially developed just for you. It makes me smile just thinking about it.

Eve's story

At sixty-five, Eve puts most people half her age to shame in terms of energy, flexibility and her positive outlook on life. Oh, and she also looks great – and at least twenty years younger than she really is. What's her secret? She's been teaching yoga for thirty years and practises what she teaches in her own time. Not a day goes by without her doing something, and it shows. The more you exercise, the younger you will look and feel.

Walk every day. Not only will you feel fitter, you'll also boost your body's natural defences against infections.

6 Sweet dreams

Ever wondered why you never seem to have a good night's sleep? You blame it on the children, your husband, your neighbours, work stress – anything but you. What if I told you that regular exercise will not only help you to relax, it will also help you sleep better at night? Think of all that glorious sleep you could be having. How much easier would life be? The world would certainly seem to be a brighter, happier place.

Are you convinced yet?

EXCUSES, EXCUSES

I'm sure you all agree that regular exercising is a sensible thing to do. Why, then, do so many of us sabotage any good intentions by wasting precious time making up excuses when we could be exercising instead? Listen to yourself:

'I don't have enough time...'
Really? Does that mean your life is so busy, you couldn't:
★ Get out of bed half an hour earlier twice a week?
★ Squeeze in a few ten-minute brisk walks during the day?
★ Park a few blocks away and walk the extra distance?
★ Run up the stairs instead of taking the lift?
★ Get off the train a stop earlier and walk or run home?
★ Alter your weekend routine so you're able to make time to exercise?
★ Hire a personal trainer who will drag you out of bed if necessary. If you can't motivate yourself, get someone else to do it for you.

No, I didn't think so – you're just being downright lazy and trying very hard to sabotage all my efforts to convince you otherwise. To be frank, it boils down to priorities – if you really want something in life you'll make time. So stop making excuses and take control of your destiny. It will give you a new lease on life and living. You will no longer feel like a victim, but victorious.

'THOSE WHO THINK THEY HAVE NO TIME FOR BODILY EXERCISE WILL SOONER OR LATER HAVE TO FIND TIME FOR ILLNESS.' EDWARD STANLEY

'I'm too tired …'

Sorry, silly me. Let me get this straight: you have no energy to exercise, but doing nothing isn't exactly going to fill you with the zest for life you need either. So how about:

★ Exercising first thing in the morning so you get it out of the way at the beginning of the day? I find this very effective. It also puts you in a good mood for the rest of the day and I find I'm more productive, too.

★ Going to bed early? If getting up earlier is a struggle, ditch the TV and hit the hay an hour earlier. You'll be amazed at the difference it makes to waking up early. Something's got to give. You can't do everything; the secret is to prioritise.

★ Being more organised? If you prefer to exercise after work, have all your kit laid out and ready for action before you're sidetracked into doing something else the minute you walk through the door. Or, have you ever thought about exercising on your way home? Commuting is dead time anyway, so why not use it to exercise – run, walk, cycle, hop; whatever suits.

★ Using your lunch break to burn some extra calories instead of just ingesting them? Getting some fresh air will help clear the cobwebs too.

It's just a matter of thinking about when you're going to exercise at the beginning of the week so you can schedule it in, and if you should have a free thirty minutes to spare – seize the moment!

'I'm just not the sporty type …'

So? I'm not suggesting we aim for Olympic Gold, but then again, why not? You don't have to be sporty to be fit. I'm no athlete. I dance round the common and my eye-ball coordination leaves much to

be desired. God was definitely on my side when I got sent to a school where athletics wasn't considered ladylike, but that didn't stop me being active. Instead of netball I did gymnastics, instead of hockey I did ballet, and when I stopped dancing I joined a gym. I always made a plan.

Exercising is not a habit or a temporary fix – it's a lifestyle, a choice or commitment you make to being healthy and keeping fit. The secret is finding something – anything – you enjoy. Perhaps you love to dance; perhaps you love spending time with your kids – so why don't you all go for a run in the park; or perhaps you love walking the dog. Your challenge is to make sure you choose something that can be easily incorporated into your daily routine. There's no point in loving to dance if you can only manage it once a month – you'll need to find another activity to top up with in between.

'Exercise is dull ...'

I agree that always doing the same thing can become monotonous, which is why I tend to change the type of exercise I do every couple of years to keep it both interesting and challenging. It also means you're constantly challenging your muscles in different ways so they don't get complacent.

Why don't you try to:

★ Start doing something you enjoy? Think of it as a fun activity rather than exercise. This will help you to get into the routine of exercising. It will also help break down some of your barriers and enable you to experience some of the benefits of exercising. Once you've got the bug, you won't look back. Remember, exercise is for life.

★ Vary your weekly routine? Instead of doing the same thing every day, why don't you do a variety of things? For example, you may choose to run on one day, take a brisk walk on another, or do a yoga class or strength training on the other. I vary my routine between yoga, Pilates, running and walking. That way I'm using a variety of muscle groups and I never get bored.

★ Join an exercise group? Whether it's a gym, a specialist exercise centre or a club. That way you will meet like-minded people who are trying to achieve the same thing as you are, and the social element makes it more fun and motivating than going it alone.

Did you know that the number of steps you take each day makes all the difference between being fat or thin? Adding 2,000 steps a day to your usual activities is enough to stop you gaining weight. Adding 10,000 can be as effective as an exercise regime. On average 2,000 steps is about one mile while 10,000 equals five miles.

'I've tried before and failed ...'

In my mind, there is no such thing as failure when it comes to exercise. You either exercise or you don't. Even if you exercise regularly, there will always be times when you manage to do more than at other times. Perhaps you've been ill, away, or just busy. The reason so many people 'fail' at exercising is, a) they have unrealistic expectations, and b) they have a bad patch and think all their efforts are wasted.

Let me ask you this. If you have a bad night's sleep – do you just give up and stop sleeping? No, you simply go to bed earlier the next night or take a nap in the afternoon to make up those lost hours. Sleeping is an integral part of our existence; without it we won't survive. In the same way, exercise needs to become part of your lifestyle. Some weeks will be brilliant, others not so good, and that's OK. Being gorgeous doesn't mean we can't be human. All you have to do is keep going and work a little harder the next time you're out. No matter how much or how little exercise you've done, it's never wasted. If the wheels fall off the cart, don't give up entirely and stomp off in a huff: tomorrow will be better. Whatever you do, never ever give up.

Eventually your body will become a finely tuned machine, and you'll find you won't be able to go more than a week without exercising. Your body will start to hunger for it – and that's when it starts to get easier.

'EXERCISE DOESN'T HAVE TO LEAVE YOU EXHAUSTED
FOR IT TO MAKE A DIFFERENCE TO YOUR HEALTH.'
MARK RICHARDSON

KEEP MOVING

To avoid hitting that brick wall try to:

★ Pace yourself. So many people wake up one day and decide to exercise. They join the gym and go all out, six days a week for a month, and then do nothing for the rest of the year. Sound familiar? The secret is to start small (like Sarah did) and build up to a more intense workout as your fitness and stamina grow.

★ When you want to give up, think about why you're exercising. Think about all the rewards you will personally reap with a little effort on your part.

★ Set yourself realistic goals. Don't commit to working out for an hour six times a week when realistically it's unlikely you'll manage more than three twenty-minute sessions. Don't worry whether you're exercising long or hard enough: the most important thing is to get yourself exercising regularly. Once you've established a routine you can set more aggressive goals and targets and fine-tune your body into shape. Trust me, that's the fun part.

BODY BUDDY

You can also call on your dream team of supporters. Exercising with a friend is much more fun. And, let's face it, on those days when you just don't feel like it, if you know you're letting someone else down, you're much more likely to make the effort.

TRY...

★ Joining a class together – go for something new or an old favourite from your youth. It doesn't have to be aerobics or yoga; it could be dancing – tap, salsa or belly, whatever grabs your attention. They're all excellent ways to keep moving and supple.

★ Going for a walk instead of a coffee.

★ Walking the dogs together – set a brisk pace and goals, like that particularly steep hill you always avoid when you're on your own.

★ Finding out about running clubs in your area – there are a growing number all over the country and you don't have to be fast or fit to begin with. Contact the Women's Running Network for more information.

★ Sharing a personal trainer. Many personal trainers will take on a small group of friends to spread the cost and encourage one another.

★ Employing a fitness instructor. Some instructors will offer group classes in your own home.

THE SHAPE YOU'RE IN

'FITNESS – IF IT CAME IN A BOTTLE, EVERYBODY WOULD HAVE A GREAT BODY.' CHER

It's a sad fact that we often want what we don't have, and body shape is no exception. So the woman with the enviably smooth stomach but equally flat boobs envies the girl with the curves; the tall cast envious glances at their more petite friends, while they in turn curse the fact that they are too short to carry off the latest catwalk trends.

As mentioned in the style chapter, what you wear can go a long way towards improving the appearance of your body shape. Clothes can definitely disguise, but only exercise can really achieve change. The important thing to remember is that every shape has its advantages and disadvantages, but by recognising your body shape you can exercise to make the most of your pros and minimise your cons.

SHAPE YOUR BODY PLAN

WORKOUT DOS AND DON'TS

THE APPLE

Your hot spots:

Your legs are often slender and shapely. You have a small, pert bottom and very sexy voluptuous chest.

Your weaker points:

You tend to carry most of your weight on the top half of your body, around the tummy, arms and chest area.

You need to:

1 Boost your cardiovascular fitness by swimming, jogging on a treadmill, short bursts on a rowing machine, skipping and speed walking, where breathing and heart rate are raised. Aim for three 30- to 40-minute sessions a week. Full body workouts such as swimming and skipping will help to tone your arms and legs at the same time.

2 Increase the fat burning potential of your output by trying to exercise over thirty minutes per session, which is when fat burning kicks in. It doesn't matter what exercise you do; anything over thirty minutes is an added bonus.

3 Increase your core strength and muscle tone by joining a Pilates or yoga class.

Failing that, try to do fifty crunches three times a week (including reverse and side as well as forward).

Try to avoid:

1 Using heavy weights on your upper body or arms; although these will tone, they can also add bulk where you simply don't need it.

THE PEAR

Your hot spots:

You have beautiful, well-defined shoulders, a slim waist and a flat tummy that most likely is completely natural and that you've never had to worry much about. In addition you've probably also got lovely slender arms and a well-defined rear end (J-Lo style).

Your weaker points:

You tend be quite flat-chested, which may or may not be a problem for you. Hips are often wider than shoulders. Bottom may be large (any extra pounds will settle here) and thighs and legs tend to be heavier.

1 Boost your cardiovascular fitness to reduce weight on hips, thighs and bottom. Aerobic exercise like jogging, speed walking and skipping are ideal. Squat jumps are a good way to tone up your legs without adding bulk. Simply stand with your legs shoulder-width apart and squat into a ninety-degree position and then jump up into the air and land back in the squat position. Do as many as you can and build up slowly.

2 Build up tone and develop the shape of shoulders and bust to help balance overall body profile. High repetition exercises like bench dips are ideal for toning up the triceps and backs of the arms.

3 Toning exercises such as Pilates and Calinetics will help tone the various muscle groups in the leg, e.g. inner thigh, calf, glutes and thighs.

Try to avoid:

1 Using heavy weights on your legs, thighs and bottom area – the idea is to tone rather than increase muscle mass. A balance between toning and cardiovascular exercise will help to avoid this.

THE STRAWBERRY

Your hot spots:

You have a cleavage that's the envy of all your friends. Your hips are narrow and your legs are long and slim.

Your weaker points:

Your shoulders and back are often quite wide, giving you a more masculine shape. Weight tends to settle on the tummy and chest area.

You need to:

1 Increase your cardiovascular output to improve fitness and help to burn fat from your waist and chest area, thereby boosting health. Shuttle runs are perfect for improving speed and agility as well as cardiovascular fitness. Simply place four markers in a line and then sprint up to the first and back again, then on to the second and so on until you've reached the fourth marker, and then repeat the sequence in reverse.

2 Tone your legs to improve tautness and shape, this will help balance out proportions and enable you to make the most of your assets.

3 Work on your core strength by doing stomach crunches (forward, reverse and side) to tone abdominal muscles and define your waist.

1 Using heavy weights on your upper body, particularly on the shoulder/chest area.

2 Swimming is excellent aerobic exercise but can accentuate and broaden shoulders. Try backstroke and remember to use your legs to power you rather than your arms.

THE RHUBARB

Your hot spots:

You're extremely fortunate in that you've probably never had to worry about your weight. Your tall, slender, willowy figure has always been envied by your female foes. You've got long slim arms and legs – what have you got to worry about?

Your weaker points:

You tend to be straight up and down and lack feminine curves. You have always desired a more defined waist and fuller chest. Your limbs tend to be long and lean but lack definition and tone.

You need to:

1 Try weight training to develop shape and definition in your bottom and legs. Squats and lunges will work on your bottom, hips and thighs. Try heel kicks, which are a fabulous way to tone and define the lower body. Simply stand tall with your hands

on your bottom. Kick your leg back until it touches your hand and then repeat with the other leg. Do as many as you're able to and increase the repetition every day.

2 Develop shapely shoulders and arms using weights and shoulder presses. Try half press-ups and tricep extensions.

Try to avoid:

1 Overdoing aerobic exercise if you're very slim. This will encourage weight loss and make you look even less shapely. Non-aerobic, strength-building exercises will give you the physique most people dream of.

THE HOURGLASS

Your hot spots:

Gorgeous feminine curves in all the right places – think Marilyn Monroe. Starting off with a cleavage to die for and a waist that's nipped to perfection. Not to mention those fabulously fertile hips.

Your weaker points:

The downside of having luscious curves is that it means you often carry a little excess weight, usually distributed evenly across your body, with particular emphasis on your arms and legs – which is where your main focus needs to be if you want to display your curves with confidence.

1 Practise stomach crunches to tone your stomach and make the most of your small waist. If you want to flaunt your assets, you need to maintain them to perfection. A flat stomach is rarely flat without a little effort. The best way to enhance your waist and keep those love handles at bay is by doing oblique stomach exercises. For example, lie on the floor holding on to your bed or a bench and bend your legs into a ninety-degree angle above your hips. Move your legs from side to side without collapsing your legs or moving your shoulders off the ground. Tough – but worth it.

2 Strengthen your upper back to improve posture, support your full chest and avoid slumping forward. Back raises are excellent for this, as are Pilates, yoga, or ballet if you have the time.

3 Shape and tone legs. Exercise your hamstring muscles to balance out large thighs: leg curls, squats and lunges are very effective.

4 Exercise arms with tricep extensions and bicep curls.

1 Overworking one area, you need to focus on boosting your cardiovascular fitness overall and whole body workouts that tone all your muscle groups to ensure you maintain a toned but curvaceous figure.

These are just guidelines to help you tailor your exercise regime to your body shape, thereby maximising its effectiveness. Remember, it's always a good idea to seek expert advice on the best exercises to maximise your full body potential.

FIT VERSUS FAT BURNING

No matter what shape you're in, the most important thing to remember is that there are two types of exercise, aerobic and anaerobic exercise.

Aerobic exercise (e.g. running, swimming or cycling) boosts your heart rate and cardiovascular fitness. This will enable you to climb stairs more easily and give you more energy to lead an active life, no matter what your age.

Anaerobic exercise (e.g. weight training, Pilates or yoga) increases muscle mass and muscle strength. The higher your muscle-to-fat ratio, the faster your metabolic rate, which will enable you to burn fat more efficiently. Anaerobic exercise is particularly important as we get older. The stronger our muscles, the less likely we are to get injured easily. Weight-bearing anaerobic exercise also helps maintain bone density to guard against osteoporosis.

When planning your exercise regime, think about the type of exercises you're doing and whether or not they're going to help you achieve the results you're looking for. If you want to be slim, then your main focus will be on aerobic exercise and burning calories. If you want to be toned and honed you're better off alternating between the two to ensure you build muscle while at the same time burning fat.

EASY RUNNING

LOSE THE LOVE HANDLES

As I've got older, one of the areas I've struggled to improve are my 'love handles'. Nothing I did seemed to recuce them. That's until I discovered running.

Now let me just get this straight – I hated running. It's never come naturally to me, but one day my husband (then boyfriend) encouraged me to go for a run with him. At first I really struggled.

I'd run a few blocks, walk a few blocks. All I could think about was the end.

Slowly, I started to get fitter, and I noticed my love handles started to get smaller – result! Now all of a sudden running looked like a very positive prospect, and I even started to enjoy it – which was a real shock for me.

What I love about running is that it's easy – you can do it anywhere, any time, any place. You're not restricted to a gym or a club; all you need is a pavement or a park. From the minute you leave your front door you're exercising, which means you save lots of time and are less likely to get distracted.

If, like me, the thought of running makes you recoil with horror, here are some tips which work for me and hopefully they'll help to get you started.

stuck in the mud?

1 *Tuned-in.* Always run to music. I got an iPod for Christmas one year and it totally transformed running for me. I now love compiling play lists to keep me fired up along the way. As soon as I feel my energy start to slow, I increase the tempo and I'm off. It also helps take your mind off the fact that you're actually running, and concentrate on the music instead.

2 **Go green.** Where possible, try to get off the pavement and into a park. I find it's so much easier to run around a park or through a field than along the pavement. Getting back in touch with nature makes it a more enjoyable and 'relaxing' experience.

3 *Keep it interesting.* If you run along the same route every day you'll quickly get bored. Do something different every couple of weeks, or run anti-clockwise around the same path.

4 **Time yourself.** The only reason I do this is because after thirty minutes of cardio activity, fat burn starts to set in. So I make sure I run for at least forty minutes to ensure ten minutes of concentrated fat burn. Kiss those love handles goodbye.

5 *Shoe perfect.* Investing in a pair of running shoes is really important. At first I refused, as I didn't think I'd keep it up, but after a year my Achilles tendons really started to hurt and I paid the price. Wearing the right shoes has enabled me to run faster and further and I couldn't recommend it more.

6 *Sprint to the finish line.* I'm one of those people who likes to pace myself when running, just in case I get tired. One thing I find really helps to accelerate your cardio fitness is to sprint the last five minutes of your run. Put every last ounce of energy you have left into it. If you're really brave you can incorporate five-minute sprints throughout your run, which will see you fit in no time.

7 *Don't stop.* No matter how tired you may feel, try to keep on going. Slowing down your pace will help your muscles to recover and enable you to get your breath back, but whatever you do, don't stop. The more you stop, the longer it will take to build up your stamina and fitness. Trust me, I learnt the hard way.

KNEES UP! LOOK AND FEEL
FABULOUS IN A WEEK

It takes one day to break a habit and seven days to start a new one. So, my friends, I've told you why, I've given you a little know-how and now it's time to snap into action. To get you kick-started I've put together a seven-day challenge, not only to get you exercising, but more than anything to get you thinking about exercise.

You have seven days, starting from tomorrow. Now don't start making excuses, we've been there, discussed it and moved on. We've identified that there's no magic time of the day or week to exercise, the secret is finding out what works for you. And the only way you're going to do that is to get started no matter what. Aim to make exercise, in whatever form, part of your everyday life. It's easy with just a little imagination and soon you won't even have to think about it.

I can't imagine my life without exercise. In fact, if I go more than a week without it, my legs start twitching and I can't sleep. Once exercise becomes an essential part of your life, like eating and sleeping, there'll be no turning back – you'll be running forwards.

Right, time for action, I want you to open your diary and plan for thirty minutes of exercise a day. I don't care if you split it into three lots of ten minutes or two fifteen-minute sessions a day. It doesn't have to be the same routine or even the same activity each day – in fact the more varied the better. I usually plan my exercise slots a couple of weeks in advance and enter them into my calendar so they become an integral part of my daily routine. That way I don't forget and get the satisfaction of ticking each session off when it's done.

To get you off the couch and into the open, I've listed a number of different things you could easily try, to give you some inspiration and hopefully get you thinking out of the box. Got your diary open? Here goes:

You can ...

1 Take the stairs, run up the escalator and avoid the lift.

2 Park further away from your destination.

3 Go for a brisk walk during your lunch break.

4 Get off the train a stop earlier and walk or – even better – run.

5 Do three sets of 20 stomach crunches while watching TV and slowly increase your reps to 100.

6 Find new routes to work, adding interest and increasing the possibilities for walking or running.

7 Get up half an hour earlier and practise some yoga.

8 Go swimming – there may even be a pool close to your office and you could swim at lunchtime or before work.

9 Walk to the shops and carry your bags back – providing they're balanced it's just like lifting weights.

10 Do your housework vigorously! A brisk session with the Hoover is as beneficial as a treadmill. And with the money you save, you could treat your fab fit figure to something new.

11 Gardening can give you a good workout too.

12 Cycle instead of driving – it's also better for the environment.

13 Think back to your childhood – hula-hoop or dance in the privacy of your own kitchen.

14 Or what about those rollerblades gathering dust at the back of the closet?

15 Buy or borrow your child's skipping rope and skip in two-minute bursts with a minute's rest in between. You'll tone your legs, arms and abs, get your heart beating and improve your overall stamina.

Oh, and don't forget to:

★ Make it fun. If it's not fun, it's not worth doing.

★ Challenge yourself and learn a new skill (kick boxing, pole dancing). That way you'll be so focused on mastering it you won't notice you're building up a sweat.

★ Ring the changes so you don't get bored. The minute it gets tedious and repetitive, it's time to try something different.

★ Think positively – but be realistic too. Baby steps: this is for life, not just on holiday.

★ Devise your own workout and set yourself targets – lunges, squats, tricep curls, crunches, press-ups, skipping – you know what you need.

…but do not hop on the scales every five minutes. This isn't about numbers, it's about a lifestyle change. You will know when you're losing weight and you will see the change in your figure as you become toned and honed. Whether you're up or down on the scale is quite frankly irrelevant – it will only unleash your demons and sabotage your efforts, and you're simply worth more than that.

Are you up for it? Seven days is all it takes. You can do this. I know it's overwhelming, but you have the willpower and potential to be gorgeous. So go on, show us what you're really made of. Flab or fabulous? You choose.

CHAPTER SEVEN

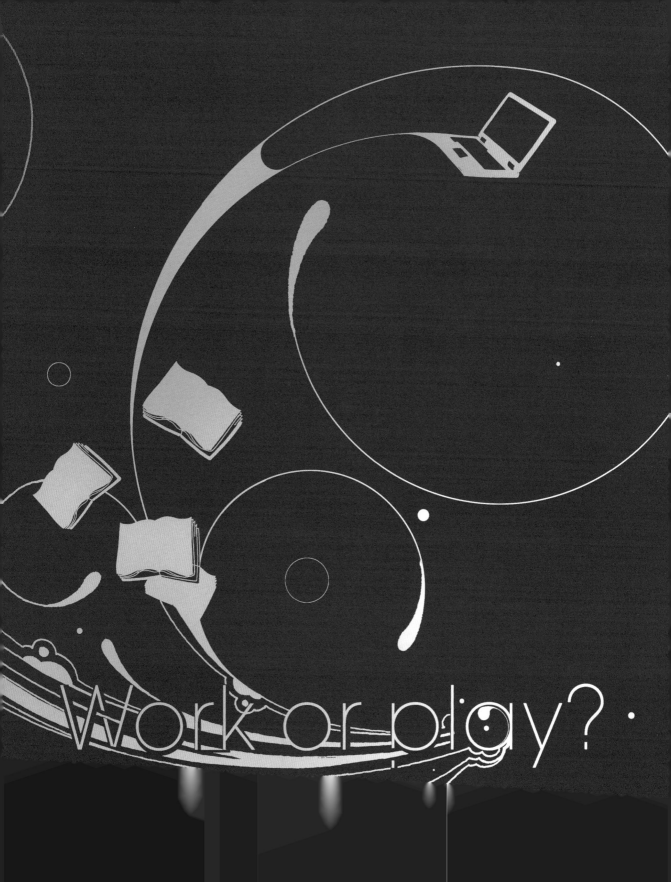

Work or play?

I WORK, THEREFORE I AM

Work is such a big part of your life and in many ways defines who you are. So where does that leave you when suddenly it's no longer there? For me, one of the hardest things about deciding to leave the corporate world was saying goodbye to the routine that defined each day. Like it or not, the commute into and out of work every day makes us feel part of something. It's a huge piece of our identity and one that's difficult to let go of. It's also one of the reasons so many people struggle with the reality of self-employment. It's not the lack of money so much as the isolation that can drive you demented.

'PEOPLE WHO BELIEVE THEY HAVE THE POWER TO EXERCISE SOME MEASURE OF CONTROL OVER THEIR LIVES ARE HEALTHIER, MORE EFFECTIVE AND MORE SUCCESSFUL THAN THOSE WHO LACK FAITH IN THEIR ABILITY TO EFFECT CHANGES IN THEIR LIVES.'
ALBERT BANDURA

I still believe I was one of the lucky ones. There are so many people out there who feel the same way I did but have not been given the paid 'holiday' to decide what they really want to do. For some this is not important – as long as you're paid well, who cares if you enjoy your job or not?

EVEN IF YOU WIN THE RAT RACE, YOU'RE STILL A RAT

If you're the type of person who wants to die knowing that you did everything you wanted to do with your life, or at least tried, then rodent status will certainly not be good enough for you. You only have one life to live. Seizing the opportunity to step off the career rollercoaster, refuel your engine, assess your life map and completely change direction if you want is incredible. I meet people every day who hate their jobs but just don't have the courage to take a risk and change their lives. Which one are you?

I'm not suggesting for one moment that starting your own business is the only option if you want to change career. But for many, including me, the challenge of creating something from scratch, being your own boss and working in an environment that inspires and interests you is very appealing and definitely worth the risks it involves. If you have a family, working for yourself also allows you to plan your work schedule to suit their needs, too. And there are clearly a lot of other like-minded people out there. I know when I was first starting out I found it very comforting to realise that I wasn't alone.

It may be that retraining is the way forward to a more rewarding career, or taking a course can be an excellent opportunity to open up new areas and expand your horizons. What feels right for you will obviously depend upon the stage of life that you've reached. For many people, women especially, having children can be a real catalyst for change and can be a good opportunity to reassess priorities and the balance between your work, family and home.

If you're returning to work after a career break you simply may not want to go back to your old job. Looking at where your interests really lie can be a stepping stone to a whole new chapter in your work life. The secret is to take the time to consider what *you* really want.

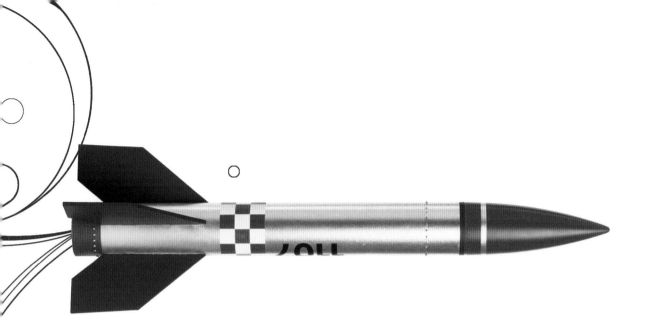

WHAT'S IN A DREAM?

Like people, dreams come in all shapes and sizes. Whether your dream is to run a successful business, go back to college, travel the length of Africa on a motorbike, live the simple life in the country, or have a family and nurture your children, the important thing is that you always acknowledge your dreams and set about making them a reality. Remember you only have one life – and the opportunity to live it is *now*. Not yesterday, not tomorrow, not some point in the future – it's now or never. Stop procrastinating and let's start creating.

One of the things that really annoys me about human nature is that we are so quick to shout 'No, it's impossible, there's no way …' and yet often we've never actually taken the time to consider the possibilities. We've written off an idea without giving it a chance. Why? Because most of us are in essence so comfortable sitting whiling away our lives that we're too scared to contemplate the possibility of something different and better. Besides, that might also make us feel guilty about the time we've already wasted.

You see, without noticing it, we're constantly dismissing the things we'd really like to do, before fully exploring all the options.

16 February 2001 – When in doubt
My alarm goes off at 7 a.m. I drag myself out of bed. Every limb in my body feels like a sack of potatoes. Another day, another week – not sure how I'm going to get through.

I feel totally and utterly disheartened and lost. I have absolutely no energy or enthusiasm for my job, but can't face looking for another one. I feel trapped – a wasteland of boredom stretches before me, and the thought of contacting recruitment agents again just makes me feel sick. All the bullshit and ra-ra they feed you and then before you know it they've sold your soul to the devil!

I feel so let down and dejected by the corporate world. All those recruitment drives when you're at university: 'We only hire the best talent', 'We'll inspire and challenge you to achieve your best potential' ... My brain feels as though it's slowly dying every day that I'm forced into the same monotonous tedium.

I finally made my way into the office and switched on my PC. In my inbox was an email from HR, 'Nicky, please could you pop in for a meeting at 10 a.m. today?' I didn't think anything of it and got down to some serious paper pushing and pencil twiddling. I almost felt slightly excited at the prospect of an appointment in my calendar. That should certainly help to speed up the day – and boy, did it!

The meeting was short and sweet. 'We're having to downsize and have had to make some "uncomfortable" decisions. Unfortunately we won't be able to offer you employment any longer but do wish you every success in the future. Of course, we'll give you a few months' salary to tide you over financially until you find a more suitable venture.'

Having now been made redundant three times, I'm well versed in the closing speech. If I'm honest, I was expecting it, but nothing quite prepares you for the moment when it comes.

BE INSPIRED

If you're reading this, you're obviously seriously considering changing your life – following a dream, doing something different, something that really sets your heart on fire, in which case you're probably wondering what to do next. Now, I could start by telling you to write a business plan, then a marketing strategy, but by this time I know you will probably have died and gone to hell rather than heaven.

I believe, in order to do anything really special in life, you need inspiration to get you started in the first place and keep you going no matter what. Inspiration is the fire that fuels your engine when you're drifting out into space, lost, not knowing where to go next. It's a tough world out there and the hardest thing is that the only person that can change your life is *you*.

'JUST DON'T GIVE UP TRYING TO DO WHAT YOU REALLY WANT TO DO. WHERE THERE IS LOVE AND INSPIRATION, I DON'T THINK YOU CAN GO WRONG.' **ELLA FITZGERALD**

Unfortunately, there is no short cut, no easy route to the top (which I assume is where you're aiming?). What really helped me was reading about other people who had been through similar experiences and had come out the other end a stronger, happier and more successful person. Now, for most of us, success is governed by our bank balance, and if we're looking to change our career, the chances are we're not doing it for a long-term pay cut. Yes, we're looking for greater job satisfaction and fulfilment, but the driving aim is often to earn more money doing something we love. However, the stories I found most inspiring along the way weren't about people who made millions, they were about survivors, people who rose above their situation to triumph in the face of adversity.

I want to share some of these stories with you as I think they will be useful inspirational resources for when the going gets tough and you're left out to dry.

Sophia's choice

For Sophia it was a personal crisis that gave her the push to start something new. Her fifteen-year marriage had come to an abrupt end and she was facing the prospect of rebuilding her life.

'It was so tempting to stick to what I knew, to carry on in the safe but dull job I'd done for years. But I knew I had to see this as an opportunity – a beginning rather than an end, otherwise I'd just feel bitter, disappointed and sorry for myself. So I did something I hadn't done for years and stopped to really think about me. What did I want? What did I enjoy? And what was I good at?

'I kept coming back to what had always been a hobby, collecting – basically brocante, anything from quilts, to tablecloths, jugs, plates, lights, anything with a quirky charm or shabby chic. So I began to research markets, I read style magazines, checked out other stores and looked at what was selling and where. Finally, four years ago I opened a shop in Cheltenham selling everything I love to buy. It wasn't an instant success but sales and the shop's reputation have grown steadily and I can now afford a full-time manager leaving me free to source stock, and visit France and other European markets regularly.

'I'm happier and so much more confident than I ever was before. And it seemed as though getting one part of my life right affected everything else, including relationships, and now I even have a new partner who enjoys travelling around on buying trips with me.'

MY G-SPOT

If there's one person who knows how to push all my inspiration buttons, it's Suzy Greaves. She's been such a constant support and inspiration to me that I thought this book wouldn't be complete without a few words of wisdom from the guru herself.

Ask the expert

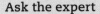 **Suzy, what's the first thing you'd tell a new client who was dissatisfied with their current career?**

I'd ask them – what had changed? Often you can be very happy in your career and then one element will change – you get a new boss or you're passed over for promotion – and then you feel fed up. It's important that you simply don't make the leap into a new career if you could make a few tweaks in your current career and be happy again at work.

Mostly we become unhappy at work – or at home – because our emotional needs aren't met. Unmet emotional needs make us feel empty, disillusioned, slightly crazy …everyone has different emotional needs – some may need control, others to be recognised, others to be approved or to be needed. It's important to recognise what your needs are, and then do whatever needs to be done to get them met. How? When you're irritable/ unhappy/discontented at work, ask yourself: what is it that I'm not getting that I need? Is it recognition? Control of a project? Respect from the boss?

Ask yourself: what can you do differently to get what you need? E.g. Do you need to talk to your boss about changing your role so you are more visible and get more recognition? Make a list of action steps to take. Then do it. You will never be happy at work if you do not learn how to get what you need from your boss and colleagues.

However, 'needs' are only half the story.

You may be unhappy at work because you simply hate the day-to-day work that you are paid to do. You may be an accountant or be in an administration role but you're innately creative. Such roles might meet your need for security but they do not light your fire. For true fulfilment at work, you need to get your needs met doing something you love.

Identify what you're naturally good at and what you enjoy. What do you do effortlessly? Are you good with people? Or good with numbers? Do you love organising or are you an ideas person? Write a list of ten talents and skills you know that you have. Now ask yourself – is your current role/job showcasing your skills and talents. If not, what would?

Many of us are often too scared to start answering that question. We've been taught to conform, and been told to put our dreams in a box because they were too 'unrealistic'. One of the first things I ask clients to do is write a 'La-La land' vision of what they would do if they didn't have to be realistic – I ask them to explore and have fun with this vision. Because I tell them it's just fantasy, it

gives the client space and room to think big and be completely unrealistic and let their dreams out of the box. And when you do that, it is incredibly powerful.

★ What are the key attributes one needs for success, or is everyone different?
Firstly define success. I would say that enjoying the journey is the greatest success. I do think that the self-help industry can peddle the idea that once you get 'there', then you'll be happy. But that is a recipe for unhappiness. If we define success as something outside of us, to get, to own, or to achieve, then we'll be forever jumping through another hoop. Have fun, create a vision or a goal, but don't put your happiness on hold until you get there. Define success by how much you enjoy every baby step towards creating a new reality for yourself. Or when the going gets tough, define success by how much you are learning as you leap outside your comfort zones.

I would say, however, that the main attribute that all my clients have is courage. People who live their dreams aren't particularly more talented or more beautiful or special – they are simply braver. They are willing to risk failure, to make themselves vulnerable, to dare to put their head above the parapet. And I applaud that.

★ Do you think it's possible for anyone to achieve their dreams?
It's possible if you believe it's possible. Because what we believe about the world is our reality. Change your beliefs and you can change your reality. Our beliefs about life and ourselves form and then come true for us when we find evidence to support our beliefs. If, for instance, you have a belief that it's not possible to live your dreams, you will probably have a barrage of evidence to show that is true – how you failed your exam, how you didn't win that competition, how nothing ever works out for you …If you want to create a new belief about yourself, let's say – 'I am quietly confident in all situations' – you must start building evidence to support that statement. Keep an evidence diary and write down three pieces of evidence a day that back up your new belief about yourself. It usually takes around a hundred pieces of evidence before a belief takes hold and your focus begins to change naturally. I know it's not very English – but affirmations can really help too. Write down a strong positive statement in the present tense: e.g. It's easy for me to achieve my dreams/earn money/find love/ be quietly confident. And say it out loud every morning. I know it can be cringy, but what you focus on expands and the more you are loud and proud about what you

want, the more your attention fixates on what you want versus what you don't want.

★ **Sometimes you know what's wrong but don't know where to go next. What advice would you give to someone looking for inspiration?**

I would challenge you if you said that you didn't know where to go next. Deep down, we all know what is right for us but often we're just blocked through fear.

I describe two voices in our heads and hearts – one is our inner pessimist who tells us to be realistic, that we're going to make a fool of ourselves; that we are not good enough to get to where we want to go. The other voice is the one I call your 'inner coach' – the one that gently encourages you, the one that speaks through intuition and gut feelings, the one that tells you that everything is possible if you just had faith. The homework that I always give my clients is to 'tune in' to their inner coach once a day until that voice becomes louder than the inner pessimist. Then you always know what to do. So for daily inspiration, let the voice of your inner coach guide you. Sit for ten or fifteen minutes a day and simply focus on your breathing or a candle flame and try to start observing your thoughts versus being in them. A week of doing this and you will start to hear the voice of your inner coach

more clearly – it's not literally a ' voice' – but more like intuitive nudges or a feeling that you should get in touch with a certain person. Trust your instincts and take action.

★ **When should reality overrule fantasy?**

If you find yourself writing your Oscar speech versus actually writing your play, you need to give yourself a little poke in the back and take some action. Coaching is actually very practical – and it doesn't work unless you take action. Often we don't take action because we are scared, so don't give yourself a hard time if fantasy is your way of procrastinating. Just acknowledge the truth and then get to the root of the fear – asking, what am I really scared of right now? Then ask, what small baby step could I take that would help me get round this fear? Research something, buy a book, ask a friend for lunch and pick their brains – choose the least scary thing you can think of. Once you've created some momentum, it's much easier to keep going. Living in fantasy versus taking consistent baby steps is just a sign you're really, really scared, so do be kind to yourself too.

★ **Changing careers is a big step – how do you know what's right for you (especially if it impacts other people like your family, for instance)?**

Often we don't allow ourselves to consider changing careers or making a big leap because we don't know how to make it happen/how we will pay the mortgage/support our families. My advice is to simply start the process and it will grow organically, as long as you keep on taking baby steps every day. A new business will often take three years to get off the ground and, for most of my clients, there is a period of six months to a year where they are doing two jobs while they transition from one career to another.

So if you do want to change career, don't do anything drastic. Just set a time period of ninety days to simply research your idea, do your business plan or get your first client at the weekend and find out if you would enjoy this new career or if you can make some money out of it. Start small, and just investigate and let your feelings guide you on whether you are on the right track. Notice any disinterest or excitement or boredom – keep focused on what excites you. Then start working with the logical mind and start putting some numbers into your business plan – could this really work?

Research the competition. What is unique or different about you? Why are you going to succeed? When you feel excited about your idea and you have a financial model that you feel might work, decide then whether you want to take the steps to transitioning into the new career – be it training or setting up the business.

★ **What advice would you give to someone going back to work after a career break or having children? Is this a good time to make changes?**
This is a bit of a 'depends' question. If it's your first baby, you can often be in shock and you're often adjusting to this whole new person in your life. I often get new mums ringing me in panic in the first three months after giving birth telling me they want to start a business right now because they can't possibly go back to working twelve-hour days and want to find a new way of working.

This is all great and very possible, but I also ask them to take it very easy in the early days of having a child as you're so sleep-deprived and exhausted that you haven't got the time or energy needed to start a whole new business. It's a great time for research and creating the idea, but I ask new mums to hang back from simply reacting to what they don't want versus coming from the place of knowing what they do want to create.

Similarly with a career break, you can often feel you don't want to go back to work because you've had a taste of what another life can feel like and you can be reacting to that versus weighing up what you really want to create.

My advice is to focus on what you want to create. Write a very detailed vision of what your new career would look like. Do you work from home or in an office? Who are your ideal colleagues? Do you work for a global empire or a cottage industry? Work on your vision until you get so excited you know exactly the kind of career you really, really want. With passion in your belly, you are halfway there. Do whatever you have to do to build a six-month financial reserve so you have the cash to cushion your move. Then write a step-by-step action plan you would need to transition from your current job through to your next career. Remember the actress Katharine Hepburn's words: 'Life is to be lived. If you have to support yourself, you had bloody well better find a way that is going to be interesting.'

★ **What are the biggest challenges you and some of your clients have faced?**
When you get pinned to the wall by your inner pessimist who tells you that you're rubbish, you're not good enough, and you were right to believe all the people who tell you that this wouldn't work.

We all have those moments. I certainly do. Something goes wrong and your inner pessimist jumps up and down on your heart and screams so loud you can't hear the other voice – your inner coach – telling you that this is simply a learning curve.

★ **What's the one piece of advice you'd give someone who's thinking about doing something different?**
Be brave.

On a personal note:
★ **How did you get to where you are today?**
Making lots and lots of mistakes and asking – what am I learning here? Being brave, finding ways to be inspired every day; and focusing on my strengths and what I am good at.

★ **What does it take to get to the top?**
Support from your friends who tell you that they love you whatever happens. A shot of unconditional love every day puts everything in perspective.

★ **What's your TDF?**
My enthusiasm.

★ **Is there anything you'd like to change about yourself?**
Do you want a list?! But I'm actually working on this point – I'm trying to get off the self-improvement treadmill and settle into some kindly self-acceptance. I no longer aspire to be perfect but I do wish I was a bit more organised and tidier sometimes!

It's all about YOU

This may be the first time in your life when you've really stopped
to think about what you want from life and where you're going next.
But before you sit back and relax, it's time for a wake-up call. Only
you can make a true success of your life, only you can alter the course
of your destiny, only you can make your dreams come true. I know,
sweetie, it sounds so tedious, but believe me it'll so be worth it when
you bump into your old boss again. There's nothing like the prospect
of revenge to get the blood pumping.

WHAT IF?

I can categorically say that these two words were one of the main driving forces preventing me from throwing in the towel and walking away – which I was tempted to do on more than one occasion. There were many times when I just couldn't take it any more. Everything I tried seemed to end in another brick wall.

The turning point came for me when friends who had always encouraged me started to question my choices. Not because they didn't believe in me, but because I was surviving on hot air. I had no money, my debts were sky-high and the black cloud of gloom hanging above me didn't look like it was going to rain opportunities any time soon. It just sat there, motionless, stifling the life force out of me. It was at this point that my friends started saying, get a job, you've tried, it hasn't worked, you need to move on, you can't go on like this. And, in all honesty, I couldn't go on like this, I was miserable.

I remember one night going home and thinking, 'OK, let's seriously consider giving up; let's consider moving on.' But all I kept hearing was, 'What if?'

What if my big break is just around the corner and I miss out? All the hard work, pain and frustration would have been in vain. I would walk away with nothing and be worse off than I was before. I was £20,000 in debt and all I could think was how long it would take to pay this off on a salaried job – when maybe, just maybe, if I got my break, £20,000 would seem like a drop in the ocean.

The thought of so much debt is probably terrifying, but please don't let that put you off. Just because you follow your dream, that doesn't mean you'll be in the same situation as I was. Circumstances are different for everyone. In a funny kind of way, the fact that I had so much debt never terrified me. Somehow, I always knew one day that cheque would come and I'd be able to pay it off in one go – and eventually it did.

However bad life might seem at this point, never forget that 'What if?' It'll be your rock and your inspiration when you need it. Anything can happen, at any time – this could be your moment but you'll never know unless you try.

WHAT DO YOU REALLY WANT TO DO?

I am offering you a licence to follow your heart and do something you really love. Go on, it's free. This is your passport to freedom and a better life should you decide to take it. But, before you rip it out of my hand – because I know you're secretly dying to – think about your current job and all the things you really dislike.

Ask yourself:
★ Is it your boss?
★ Would changing jobs be the solution or is the commute the problem?
★ Do you simply hate having to travel into an office every day?
★ Or is it the type of work you do?
★ Perhaps switching companies isn't the answer as you would simply be doing the same thing somewhere different.
★ Do you enjoy your job but want more flexibility, perhaps working part time to spend more time at home with your family?
★ Would working freelance be a possibility, giving you control over when and how much you work?
★ Or are you thoroughly frustrated and fed up, and need a complete change to get your juices flowing again?

Once you've narrowed down the issues, it's much easier to think practically about the environment you'd like to work in and the type of job you'd like to do. When you've considered this, think about your values. What is important to you? What do you fundamentally believe in? It may be that ethical or environmental issues are vital for you, or working to support a cause. Perhaps the most important thing for you at the moment is to be there when your children come home from school. Whatever you value, finding a career or job that fits in with it will go a long way to determining just how happy you feel.

One of the things that is really important for me is to do something that helps people feel better about themselves. So, although I'm passionate about fashion, working on a fashion magazine or in a fashion house wouldn't help me fulfil this need. Therefore, even if you are passionate about doing something, you need to make sure it fits in with your values, as you are then more likely to be yourself and excel at doing it.

'YOUR ASPIRATIONS ARE YOUR POSSIBILTIES'
SAMUEL JOHNSON

NATURAL TALENT

We've all got it. Each and every one of us is naturally talented at something; in fact most of us have natural talents in places we haven't even begun to discover yet. The more adventurous our lives, the bigger our journey of self-discovery and the more likely we are to unleash our talents. For instance, I had no idea I had the ability to put pen to paper until I started my own business and was constantly asked to write columns or features for magazines. Tapping into fashion unleashed my creative spirit, which had been suppressed by the City for so long. Had I never changed direction and followed my dream, I might never have discovered it.

'What are you good at?' I remember that was one of the first things Suzy (my life coach) asked me when I was at a loss as to what to do next.

'Not sure,' was my initial response, followed by, 'I think I'm quite good at styling people'.

'Great, so what could you do around that?'

And the rest is history. You see, as soon as I started to tap into my natural talents, my creative juices started to flow, and I started to attract opportunities that I would never have considered before.

What I'm trying to say is, if you're scared of heights but your dream is to jump out of a plane, go for it – just don't make a profession out of it, unless you find a new calling in life. Doing something you're naturally good at is half the battle won. I'm not suggesting you can just sit back and enjoy the ride; you'll still have to work hard, but it will be a lot easier and much more pleasurable.

So have you got enough to think about? Are your dream juices starting to flow and take shape? I hope so, because I'm so excited for you. This is the beginning of an exhilarating journey and I feel honoured to be on board while you take the ride.

Now you have your dream the next step is … what exactly do you *intend* to achieve?

I INTEND TO . . .

You now have the big picture, you know where you're heading, but what do you want it to look like? What are the specifics, or, in other words, your intentions? And this does not mean what should it look like or what would other people expect. I mean what do you want to do? You're the one with the courage and determination to follow your dream and so you must define the parameters.

Whilst 'sunning' myself under a parasol, smothered in factor 30, on a beach in Mauritius, unemployed, and with little to no prospects as far as I could see, I designed my ideal career, which I intended to look like this:

★ I want to do something with fashion and clothes.
★ I see myself running my own company.
★ I want to earn enough money to be able to afford the lifestyle I wish to have (including the perfect husband, house in the country, holidays abroad …not much then, but hey 'Go Big or Go Home' I say).
★ I would like to be well known and well regarded in my field of expertise.
★ I see myself being in the public eye (not all the time) but being interviewed by the media because of my achievements and giving speeches/talks at functions to inspire people.

★ I see myself as being powerful with a lot of responsibility in a positive sense.
★ I want to absolutely love my job. I want to build a career that rivals all the jobs and companies I've worked for.
★ I want to be loved and respected by my friends, colleagues and family.
★ I want to do something that really challenges and inspires me. I want to prove to all those around me that I can make it, and that I am special …one day I'll be famous …watch this space! (Yes, I actually wrote this – sad but true).

For the record, I'm feeling a little freaked out right now. I haven't read these notes for years and am amazed, to say the least, at how close to reality they've become. In fact, this is my reality. I can honestly say, hand on heart, that I didn't for one moment expect that it would be, back then, when all I had was belief that there was more to life than a dull job and a pay cheque.

CLEAR THINKING

Talking from experience I know that being really specific about how you want your dream to 'look' will help create your reality.

★ Decide what works best for you. For me, it's writing a description of exactly what I'm looking for and what I intend to be doing.

★ For others it may be creating a visual chart with cuttings of places you'd like to visit or people you'd like to meet.

★ The more you understand what it is you're aiming for, the clearer you'll be about what you don't want to do.

This list or chart can also be an inspiring resource to refer back to when you hit a low and need to remember just what it is you're aiming for.

Without a list of intentions, you can still get where you want to go if you have enough determination, but the journey will be longer as you struggle to identify what it is you really want. If you clearly establish this at the outset you'll have a more visible aim and a stronger sense of purpose.

HUNGRY FOR MORE

The whole way along your journey, you must expect to be challenged and tormented beyond your imagination. Look what Richard Branson went through to save his airline, or Lance Armstrong to win the Tour de France, not just once but seven times.

Just because you have a dream, doesn't mean it's going to be an easy ride. You have to be prepared to make sacrifices – and some will be easier than others. The question is: where will you draw the line?

I know I used to taunt myself and say, 'Oh well, if it gets to the point where I can't afford to pay my mortgage, then I'll just have to give up.' And guess what – that exact thing happened, but instead of giving up I moved out and rented out my flat.

'If I get so broke I won't be able to feed myself, then I'll have to give up.' And that happened too, but still I didn't give up, I simply got a part-time job.

'I'll give it another six months, and if things haven't picked up by then, I'll give up.' I'm still here six years later despite the fact that there were plenty of rocky times along the way, so that ultimatum failed to work either.

We conjure supposedly awful scenarios in our heads about the worst things that could possibly happen, and the funny thing is they often do, but if you're really committed you will find a solution. The vital factor is to be hungry; you have to feel so passionately devoted to your dream that nothing and no one will deter you from your mission.

I think one of the challenges, when you're making a total career change, that you don't consider when you're starting out, is that it becomes all-consuming, which can be quite hard on those around you, but it's simply not possible to be anything less. You have to live, breathe and feel the dream.

FAMILY MATTERS

It may be that this level of commitment is impossible for you at this time. When you are thinking about making changes, you have to be realistic about the impact on partners and children and how they will feel. It's not impossible, but you need to consider how daily life could still function. If you're just going to be stressed about time away from your children, you're never going to feel truly committed or happy. Perhaps one answer is to call on your dream team for extra support. You may be able to help one another with childcare, so no one has to lose out as you follow your dream.

One of the main motivators for many women to change jobs is to give them greater flexibility and time at home. If this is the case for you, be realistic about it. There may be other good options that will help you have it all – a satisfying career and quality time with your family. Investigate the possibilities of working part time or freelance, or perhaps by working a longer day you can take an afternoon off each week, or even work from home on one or two days. Employers are increasingly aware of the needs of working parents. Take the plunge: you'll never know unless you ask.

Art for art's sake

Liz read English at university and went on to work in publishing. Though she had never studied art, the subject had always interested her. 'My office was really close to St Martin's and I used to see the art students drifting out. I was a bit envious and curious about what art school was really like.'

It was the sudden death of her father that prompted her to finally find out. 'It's such a cliché, but going through Dad's papers and looking at old photos made me stop and think. Life's short and there's no point wondering what if…or maybe I could have done that? I finally stepped inside St Martin's and found out exactly what I needed to do to get onto a foundation art course. It was actually all very straightforward and almost before I knew it I was enrolled. It has changed my life. I'm now in my third year of a part-time art course. I need to work a couple of days a week to help pay fees, but I really love it and know this is where my future lies.'

TIME BOMB

You've done it! You've taken the plunge and are following your dream to do something different. You're fired up and ready to go. Well done – this is the beginning of the rest of your life, a totally new you. Your first few weeks are busy with networking, marketing and promoting your idea. Everyone's excited, particularly you. This feels great and you wonder why you didn't do it sooner.

But then … The initial euphoria slowly starts to ebb away as you will the phone to ring and the bookings to pour in. You start to lose motivation as you're constantly pushed to come up with new ideas and try out something different to bring the business in. You find yourself nostalgically longing for those days at work where you had the luxury of doing nothing because you're feeling slightly worse for wear after a big night out, knowing that your pay cheque would appear anyway. You miss the chitchat with colleagues over the coffee machine. This is when the penny drops and you realise it's all up to you and you have to come up with a game plan if you're going to make this work.

It was at this point that I decided to embark on some PR.

I remember when I got my first magazine feature, a four-page spread in *Shape* magazine. The title was 'Dress Me a Stone Lighter'. I had to find four case studies of various shapes and sizes and style them to look slimmer.

It all went like clockwork and I remember being so excited when the piece came out that I didn't want to go out for fear I'd miss a call. I bought countless copies (probably half the print run, silly me) to show to all my friends. I was convinced this was going to be the turning point and my big break. Bearing in mind I'd only been running my own style company for four months, I had a lot to learn. I imagined the phone would ring off the hook and I wouldn't be able to keep up with all the business the article would generate.

I sat in my flat all day until eventually at 3 p.m. I got a call from a potential customer, who turned into a client. How exciting! This was the beginning…

I never got another call – that was it. All that effort for a single booking. I can't tell you how deflated I felt. To think I'd been reluctant to do any publicity in the first place. Well, I was a little naïve in those days.

'GENIUS IS ONE PER CENT INSPIRATION AND NINETY-NINE PER CENT PERSPIRATION.'
THOMAS EDISON

When you psyche yourself up, do all the right things and nothing works, it can be soul destroying at times. Here are some of the lessons I learned the hard way:
★ Do not expect things to happen instantly.
★ Do not expect the money to roll in overnight or even in the first year.
★ It doesn't matter how much or how little money you have, you can't buy acceleration, you simply have to sit it out.

TREADING WATER

Over the years I have cultivated the patience of a saint. It's a bit like treading water: you're performing all the right actions, but you just don't seem to be going anywhere. Don't get disheartened; this is all part of the process, the true test of your staying power.

The worst thing is desperately waiting for something to happen. When things seem to grind to a halt and you don't know what to do next. I suggest you take a break and do something totally different. There are times when you just need to surrender to the universe and 'give up' for the day.

★ Go to the gym, visit a friend, go to a movie, read a book, visit a gallery.
★ Do something that will take your mind off your business and switch you back into creative mode again.
★ You will come back refreshed with a new sense of perspective on a clear path forward.
★ You need mental space to be creative.

Sometimes it's not in the doing that we find the answers but when we do nothing.

PEOPLE ROCK

Imagine a world where the only person in it is you. Think of all the opportunities at your disposal, the lack of queues, no traffic, no waiting lists for the latest must-have handbag, no pollution. But that would also be a place where there's no one to make you laugh, no one to give you a hug at the end of a bad day, no one to give you a kiss to make it better. The point is, people make our lives worth living, but they can also make it a living hell. It depends entirely on who you surround yourself with.

When you're charting new territory and embarking on a totally new direction, you need to be tough and very choosy when it comes to the people you surround yourself with. The wrong people will jump on your enthusiasm and crush your spirit. They will make you question and doubt your choices; they will kill your passion and leave you feeling empty and deflated – to the point where you may even give up. This might seem overly dramatic, but the people around you really will play a vital part in whether you succeed or fail.

WHAT'S IN A NAME?

When I decided to call my business Tramp2Vamp!, everyone was horrified. The only person who thought it was a good idea was Suzy. She thought it was fantastic and I can still hear her enthusiastic scream. In fact, that's all I needed to hear, and the only thing I listened to when everyone else started questioning and doubting my decision.

It's quite incredible, really, how people you hardly know feel compelled to give you their penny's worth of advice, which for me involved something along the lines of, 'I don't think that's a very good name. I mean, who wants to look like a tramp?'

That's not to say that just because Suzy agreed with me, she was right. No one can tell you what's right or wrong, what will work and what won't. The truth is, if you're forging new ground, you need to find out for yourself. You're not looking for answers, just reassurance and support. Knocking you down is not going to benefit anybody.

At first, other people's opinions really affected me, and I would have serious doubts as to my choices, but my core believers would always set me right. All I had to do was pick up the phone and they'd simply put me back on the straight and narrow. Eventually, I became hardened, and realised that the people who questioned me simply didn't get what I was doing and were never likely to fall into my target audience. For instance, people who got it, loved it, and saw it for what it was. Of course no one wants to look like a Tramp, and not everyone wants to look like a Vamp – but to be transformed from a Tramp to a Vamp conjures up images of Cinderella and her Prince – it's a fairy tale; something we all secretly aspire to.

Six years on, no one even questions it any more; it's just a brand name, in the same way as Virgin is (apart from the fact that I'm not a billionaire…yet). When you think of Virgin, you think of the branding, you don't start thinking about what the word 'virgin' actually implies.

People can be cruel, and when you're treading on uncertain ground, a sweeping comment can undermine your confidence.

Thinking back, the majority of times when I've truly questioned and doubted myself have always been as a result of other people's remarks. People can lift you up or throw you down. The secret is to be selective about who you open up to and spend your precious time with.

SOLID AS A ROCK

Only surround yourself with people who really care about you. Whether that's one person or five, you simply can't afford anything less. Think of them as your champions. They will be your rock, your foundation to help, nurture and support you through your journey and beyond; in other words, your dream team.

GUT FEELING

Thinking back to the altercations I had over calling my business Tramp2Vamp, Suzy and my close friends supported me through the wobbles, but one of the main reasons I never faltered was because my gut feeling told me it was right.

I still remember the day when I had my 'light-bulb' moment, as Oprah would say – cheesy, but effective. I was sitting chatting to a friend sipping a glass of wine on the King's Road. I was explaining my struggle to come up with a name for my business that was catchy, unique and – more importantly – for which I could buy the dot-com. Seems quite irrelevant now, but you have to remember that in those days I was all about global domination. So owning a dot-com was simply critical as far as I was concerned.

Anyway, my friend started saying something about the Lady and the Tramp and it just clicked – Tramp2Vamp! I knew the name was right. I rushed home, checked the URL and the dot-com was available. I took that as a sign.

I knew I was on to something. I can't explain how but I just knew. This is what I call my gut feeling. It's an intrinsically powerful force that lies within all of us, though some of us tap into it more than others. It's our internal protection system. It gives you a red light when something's not right and a brilliant green one when you're on the right track. It's like meeting Mr Right – when everyone says you just know. So irritating when you're obviously not in the know.

From that point on, I started tapping into my gut feeling more and more. It's such a powerful force that it makes you feel in charge of your destiny instead of floating breathless and directionless through thin air. I always know if something's wrong or if it's not going to happen. It's almost as if I'm able to prepare myself for disappointment beforehand, so that when it does happen, it's a softer fall.

Your gut feeling is a powerful sensor when it comes to assessing other people. When I meet someone new, I can immediately discern whether or not they're genuine, whether or not they have my interests at heart and whether I want to work with them. I use this sense when I'm recruiting new staff: it's not so much the credentials that sway my judgement as my gut feeling. The odd time when I've gone with credentials, they've caused me no end of problems. Once again my gut feeing has always been right.

I'm not the only one

Alex James is best known as the bassist with Blur, though as anyone who has read his newspaper columns or listened to him on Radio Four will know, he is now also a sheep farmer and cheese maker. This came about almost by accident when he and his wife were looking for a new home in the Cotswolds. His story really illustrates my own feelings about how important it is to follow your instincts.

He often writes about the farm for his weekly column in the *Independent*:

'I remember the feeling I had when I walked into my very first, tiny, rented flat in Covent Garden – an overwhelming sense that this place must be mine…when you get the feeling of not wanting to leave – that's your home. At the farm … I knew I was having that feeling.'

Not everyone else shared his enthusiasm; in fact most were appalled and felt it was their duty to advise against the move. 'But my wife and I thought, no – we knew, that it was now or never. We'd glimpsed a version of paradise and nothing was going to stop us. We bought the place and, although I still love spending time in London, I do feel ready for something else now.'

And when you're in the right place for you, it seems other things slot easily into place.

FORCE IT

I urge you to tap into this incredible inner force within you. Use it as your judgement call whenever you're unsure about anything. It gets you out of all sorts of otherwise embarrassing or humiliating situations and, who knows, it could even save your life. It also gives you that much needed reassurance when everything seems to be going wrong – that you are in fact on the right track.

FEARLESS AND FANCY FREE

The thing that stops you from making changes is you. Fear governs our lives. It's the natural warning system that you're in danger, that you're taking risks. When we feel it, our natural instinct is to run and hide. The older we get, the more we understand the consequences of our actions and the bigger our fear of taking risks becomes.

Fear is an incredibly complex emotion. On the one hand it can be invigorating and the catalyst that drives the adrenaline pumping through your veins. On the other hand it can be utterly paralysing. When fear becomes too big for your mind to process, your brain literally gives up, which is why you tend to feel so utterly helpless and lost. But nothing quite beats that feeling of satisfaction and pride when you conquer your fears and achieve something against all odds. Which is why a little bit of fear in our lives is perfectly healthy. Use fear to your advantage, but don't let it control your actions and choices in life. The minute it does, you're history, and your life will become monotonous and dull.

The positives ...
The good thing about fear is that it keeps you in check. When you feel it, you know you're being challenged. When you beat it, you know you've succeeded. You've taken a step closer to achieving your dream – which is so exhilarating it's worth the risk and stress you went through to achieve it.

The negatives ...
So if fear can be such a positive influence on our lives, what are we so scared of? It's when fear starts to take over your life and prevent you from moving forward that it becomes more of a negative influence. This is when it's important to tackle your fears head on by taking small steps to overcome them.

Luckily for most of us, we don't just have one fear, we have many.

These fears are made up of what I call demons, which sit on our shoulders whispering derogatory comments into our ears every day. It's quite extraordinary really, if anyone else was as harsh to me as I can be to myself, I think I'd curl up and die. We – or certainly I – have the potential to make a mountain out of a molehill, taking something relatively insignificant and converting it into a drama of massive proportions.

For example, a series of events could look something like this:
★ I email some copy over to a client for them to review and get no feedback.
★ I start to panic that they don't like it.
★ I start to worry that they're really disappointed with my work and won't want to work with me again.
★ After all, I'm really no good at writing, I start to tell myself.
★ That's probably why I got made redundant so many times; they've seen through me too.
★ I'm really no good at anything, not sure why they wanted to work with me in the first place.

★ I should have worked harder; perhaps then I would have got it right.
★ I'm such a failure, not sure why anyone would want to spend time with me. And so it goes on.

You might laugh, but I know I'm not alone here! We all spend a good proportion of our lives worrying about trivial things that often never actually happen.

I don't believe we ever truly conquer all our demons and fears. They are an integral part of our transformation journey. The difference between those who succeed and those who fail is not a question of luck; it's the acceptance that there is in fact no difference. Failure is in essence … success!

Singles, spouses and significant others

CHAPTER EIGHT

'LIFE IS PARTLY WHAT WE MAKE IT AND PARTLY
WHAT IT IS MADE BY THE FRIENDS WE CHOOSE.'
TENNESSEE WILLIAMS

Relationships are always an important part of life. And I mean all relationships – friendship, love, marriage, relationships by choice, relationships by birth. You may be wondering what your relationships have to do with changing your life. Well, I would argue that the way you relate to your partner (or lack of one), friends and family has everything to do with the way you see yourself, and how you deal with challenges, influencing the rest of your life and ultimately affecting your ability to change and fulfil your destiny.

And the relationship we probably agonise over most from the time our hormones first start raging as teenagers until we are all supposedly grown up, is finding the perfect partner. Someone who loves us for ourselves, who appreciates all our little foibles, who wants to spend time with us and, it goes without saying, someone who will support and be there for us. But as overheard conversations on the train, at work, in the playground and the plotlines of numerous novels and Hollywood films all testify – this is one relationship that is rarely without trauma, twists and tantrums.

singles, spouses and significant others

WANTED - MR RIGHT

I was always the single one. My friends went from one serious relationship to another; they got married, populated our planet with little fingers and toes, and still I remained the odd one out at the dinner party. 'Shame, poor Nics – no man, no money…how does she survive?' Er, hello there girls, the only reason I'm single is because you keep setting me up with snivelling, snotty men who couldn't swat a fly! Do I look desperate?

The truth is, I might have felt it, but I sure didn't look it. A lot of time and effort went into cultivating this air of confidence, you know. Not only that, I had a plan. I knew exactly what kind of man I was after, and I wasn't about to settle for anything less. Although, if I'm really honest, my thirtieth birthday had come and gone and I was starting to feel a little anxious that perhaps expecting Mr Right to pitch up on my doorstep might be a little ambitious.

I decided to grab the bull by the horns and once again take control of my destiny in the only way I knew how – by trying to control it. First stop – 'Only Lunch', or dinner or whatever takes your fancy… just no sex required. In other words, a dating agency wrapped up in various gastronomic expletives so that no one ever has to know what you're doing. After all, it's Only Lunch.

It sounded ideal to me. All I had to do was describe what kind of man I was looking for and they'd come up with their closest match. Not being a particularly fussy person, or so I thought, there should be countless specimens to choose from. All this convenience for the small price of a *whole month's rent*?! All of sudden, the idea of an arranged marriage sounded like a good investment.

Needless to say, by this stage I was so suckered in at the prospect of all the perfect men I'd have at my disposal, my credit card was on the table before I could blink.

WE HAVE A MATCH

How exciting – my first date. I was filled
with eager anticipation for what I was
convinced would be their closest match
to my perfect man. I'll never forget
walking into the restaurant that evening
(so much for lunch, but I was a busy lady
and this was Mr Right, so he deserved
a bit of time). As I was led to the table,
time stood still.

It was a train wreck of an evening.
My hope of meeting Mr Right was fading
rapidly. Determined not to give up, I went
on a few more dates – after all, I had to
get my money's worth.

One asked me to stand up as the last
person he met looked slim sitting down …
Another thought I was his soul mate
when I casually mentioned Scotland was
beautiful – very odd. And another told me
how he couldn't stand ambitious women
and was only looking for a domestic
goddess to cook and clean his house,
which certainly wasn't me. So eventually
I gave up.

SPEED IT UP

But not for long. Next up was speed-
dating. It sounded ideal: five minutes
and you're done. Tick or no tick and move
on. Perfect. After all, it only takes a first
impression, not a laborious lunch. This
was going really well. Everyone I'd met
seemed really nice, yes tick; I'd meet up
with him and him and him again. By the
end of the evening, I'd ticked fourteen
men, and – surprise, surprise – they'd
all ticked me. Nightmare! I then found
myself drowning in semi-blind dates (a
five-minute chat doesn't really count as
a date), night after night, and not one of
them improved on their five-minute chat.

singles, spouses and significant others

Through all of this rigmarole, the one thing I never lost sight of was exactly what I was looking for. I had my checklist etched onto my brain. Yes, I went on lots of first dates but I never went on a second unless they were serious contenders for Mr Right. I knew what I wanted and I was gonna get him... The only question was: where?

WHEN YOU LEAST EXPECT IT

When Fran, a new recruit in our PR office, asked me to describe my ideal man, I didn't have any problems spelling it out.

My Mr Right

★ Must have biceps – which should narrow down the UK population considerably, don't you think?
★ Must be tall – anything over six foot
★ Must have a good sense of humour
★ Must be intelligent
★ Must be healthy – not a fast-food junkie
★ Must be active – do lots of sport
★ Non-smoker
★ Preferably dark hair
★ Hair on chest but no hair on back or bum (I know – it's unlikely she'd know anything about that, but had to throw it in)
★ Don't mind younger, but not too old
★ Not threatened by ambitious women

At the end of my long list, the entire office was staring at me open mouthed in disbelief. But as I turned back to my PC, Fran piped up. 'I think I know just the man for you.'

Having just survived a barrage of blind dates, I was in no hurry to go on another.

That was Monday. On Thursday night that same week, after some email correspondence with mystery man, confirming that he did in fact own a pair of biceps, I set off to meet him for a drink.

'Green shirt by the door,' he texted. Well, that didn't exactly give me a lot to go on. Let's hope no one else is wearing green tonight, I thought as I texted him back: Blonde hair and glasses en route.

I eventually married the green shirt by the door and have never looked back. The relationship you have with your partner has a huge influence on the rest of your life. In fact, I'd go so far as to say that, without Rob, I don't think I would have achieved as much as I have. Not because he helped me do it, but he gave me the foundation and freedom to be who I am and do what I do best – no questions asked. It's really important to get it right, as this is one decision that will impact the rest of your life.

If you're really serious about finding true love, you have to take strategic action.

MY FIVE-STEP PLAN FOR FINDING MR RIGHT:

1 *Know what you want*

It's very hard to reach a destination if you don't know where you're aiming in the first place. The same goes for finding Mr Right. If you don't know who you're looking for, you won't recognise him when he eventually crosses your path. I know this probably doesn't sound very romantic, but trust me it works.

Make a list, in detail, of the man you're looking for. What he looks like, what he does, where he lives, his interests – anything you can think of. The more specific, the more likely you are to identify him. None of this, I'm not very fussy, anything will do, because that's simply not true and you know it.

You see, I believe that the reason most of us take so long to find The One is because we invest too much energy going out with men who we know deep down in our heart aren't right, but we're too scared to be on our own.

Instead of investing precious time and energy tracking him down, we get suckered into compromising on someone that's not even close to second best.

Being really clear in your mind about who you're looking for will ultimately save you a lot of time and emotional energy. Once you've drawn up your profile of Mr Right, as with all your life intentions, hide it somewhere safe and wait for things to happen.

singles, spouses and significant others

'DON'T SETTLE FOR A RELATIONSHIP THAT WON'T LET YOU BE YOURSELF.' **OPRAH WINFREY**

2 Trust in yourself ... there's a lid for every pot

Call me sentimental, but I truly believe there is someone special out there for each and every one of us. The problem is that most people haven't got the patience to find him. Perhaps your biological clock is ticking, your friends are all married, you thought you'd found him before only to have the relationship go sour, or you're just lonely. Our emotions often encourage us to get involved in relationships for the sake of being in a relationship, rather than the person themselves. You have no control over when you'll meet Mr Right; you just have to trust that he's out there. Like setting up your own business, when you start out, you have no idea whether it will be successful or not, you just have to trust in yourself and your dream. The same philosophy applies to finding your Mr Right. No matter how many dud dates I went on (and there were loads), I never lost sight of the type of person I was looking for. That's not to say I didn't get disheartened or despondent, of course I did, but that's where your list of intentions comes in.

3 Change your jungle

You need to approach finding Mr Right in the same way you would look for a target audience for your product. If one strategy's not working, you need to find another. As much as you may like your smug married friends, it's unlikely you're going to bump into a hot single bloke while watching DVDs in their sitting room – it's time to change your jungle. Do something different. Try out a new bar, take up a hobby, or go on an active holiday where you can meet like-minded people with similar interests to you. For example, hiking, yoga, tennis, dancing, Italian cookery – the options are endless. If nothing else, you'll make some new friends who could introduce you to a new circle of people. Sometimes the most random encounters can lead you to your destiny. The question is random or fate? You decide. Follow your heart, believe in your intentions and fate will play right into your hands.

4 Focus, focus, focus

Never, ever compromise. You know what you want, so go out and find him. Why settle for second best when you can have it all?! Aren't you worthy of the very best? You have to believe in yourself and your worth. If you don't honestly believe you'd get a second glance from your ideal man, you've got some work to do. Go back to the exercise, nutrition and style chapters in this book and get motivated. Yes, you. If you're really serious about finding your dream man, you've got to stop dreaming and get focused. Best place to start is with yourself - get in shape, sort out your hair and, as for your wardrobe: need I say more? Creating opportunities in life is all about creating a positive aura around you. Remember my 'Falling in Love' theory? (See page 46.) The secret to success is being able to switch on this feeling without falling in love. When you're down in the dumps, fed up, lonely and miserable with life, you will be surrounded by a vacuum of inertia. The energy around you is stagnant and as a result nothing happens and no one calls.

This is when you need to take control and switch your aura from black to red. Why? Well, to be perfectly frank, you're not going to meet anyone when you're in this space.

How? Go out and do something that makes you happy or puts a smile on your face. Play your music full blast and dance around the room; go for a run and pump up those endorphins; go to the movies; meet up with a friend; pack your bags and hit the highway – see where it takes you. Try anything that will diffuse the negative energy around you and switch it to something more energised and positive. The better you become at doing this, the easier it will become to manage those days when life seems like a lot of effort for little reward. It's these days when we often give up on our dreams and compromise on someone else. That's why it's so important to have a back-up plan for the low times, so you can quickly get back on top before they zap the energy out of you.

'THE MOST IMPORTANT THING IN LIFE IS TO LEARN
HOW TO GIVE OUT LOVE AND TO LET IT COME IN.'
MORRIE SCHWARTZ

So are we back on track? Brilliant! Now start to focus on how you can get yourself looking and feeling fantastic – refer back to Chapters 3 & 4 for hot tips on how to maximise your assets. It's not a coincidence that most women meet their dream man when they're not looking. The reason they're not looking is because they're enjoying life and content within themselves. Once you get to a place of self-confidence, compromise won't come into the equation.

5 *Gut instinct*
You've probably figured out by now that, whether you're after a new body, a new career or a new man, the principles of achieving success are pretty much the same. Know what you want, make a list of intentions, believe in your dream and – last but not least – trust your instincts.

Think of the hours and hours we spend analysing a conversation, a text, an email, when, although it's comforting to do so, more often than not we know the answers ourselves. Sometimes I think back on the number of occasions I knew a relationship wasn't going to work out, but I desperately wanted it to. I'd feel sick to my stomach with nerves and stress, when if only I'd listened to my instincts and let it go, instead of trying to make it work, I would have been home and dry a lot quicker and on to the next one.

Our gut instincts are our most powerful tool. If something or someone doesn't feel quite right – *move on!*

There, I've said it. It's out and there's no going back. How many times have you wanted to tell a friend exactly that, but didn't have the heart? Well, take it from me – sometimes honesty can be truly liberating.

MEETING MR RIGHT

So where do people meet their Mr Right? Interested to know, I started to ask. Not surprisingly, lots of couples met at college or work, some even at school, but there were others …

'At the station on my way to work when all the trains were cancelled. We started talking, then walking. We shared a cab, swapped telephone numbers, had a drink together that night and haven't stopped seeing each other since.'

'I lost an oar in the middle of a boating lake and Mark rescued me! He's made a career of it.'

'I'd recently broken up with my partner. Feeling fragile, lonely, and as if I'd never meet anyone again, I agreed to spend a week in the Lake District with my family. I like hiking and decided to climb Scafell. When I reached the summit, Nick was just standing there … almost as if he was waiting for me. I don't believe in love at first sight but we both knew there was a connection. It was a really romantic way to meet.'

'It was my first day at work and I was feeling very nervous. I literally ran into Tim on the stairs and he directed me to my new office and made me a cup of coffee.'

'During my second year at university I returned late to my hall of residence in time to see a very tall man wearing stockings and suspenders fall out of my neighbour's room. I helped him up and he introduced himself. Not the most promising start (though it was only fancy dress), but he was very funny and clever and I like men who make me laugh. He's also got great legs!'

'We had children in the same class and had met before, but we began talking at a parents' evening, waiting to see the form teacher who was running late. Neither of us was looking to meet anyone after going through painful divorces. Because we're both parents we understand the problems and the baggage that comes second time around.'

The point is, you never know when Mr Right is going to stumble or fall across your path. Knowing what you're looking for will help you cut to the chase so you don't end up tripping over the opportunity of a lifetime.

RIGHT OR WRONG?

Friends always used to tell me you know you've met The One when it's easy. No stress, no analysis, like wrapping yourself up in a double tog feather duvet.

That didn't sound particularly appealing to me. What happened to fatal attraction, a passion so powerful no amount of personal resolve could keep you away; chemistry as strong as a lightning bolt?

The truth is, I've experienced all of those, and – to be perfectly honest – they're bloody hard work, not sustainable long term and usually end in tears. It's very easy to mistake sexual attraction for your Mr Right. The thing with attraction is that it can very quickly get addictive. The more you have the more you want and, slowly but surely, you start to lose your resolve and self-confidence as you desperately cling on to what's become your 'happy drug'. This will slowly chip away at your self-esteem until you start to lose your sense of self and can only be identified by the negative relationship you're in.

The reality is that your relationship died a death months ago, or perhaps it never really got off the ground, but you think it's easier to stick with what you know than face being single again. It's time for a wake-up call. Take a good look at yourself – you're probably not half the person you used to be. What happened to your party spirit, your carefree nature, your spontaneous charm?

A good relationship is with someone who 'Gets You' – who totally understands how you tick. I've lost count of the number of boyfriends I've had who thought I was crazy. Sometimes it really got me down and I used to wonder if perhaps they were right. In fact, I wasn't the problem (well, of course not!): they simply didn't get me or were intimidated by me. Either way, it wasn't a good fit. When I did eventually meet Mr Right, it was such a relief to be able to be myself and not have to worry about what he thinks of me day and night. I could just *be*, and do what I do best, which is being *me*.

SIFT OUT THE DEAD WOOD

One of the reasons why people are too scared to change an aspect of their lives is because it often opens up a can of worms. Have you ever thought how difficult or impossible it is to be successful in changing one aspect of your life when another area's dragging you down? Think about it. If your job makes you feel low and depressed, you're not going to be oozing sex appeal and confidence on a night out on the town so, realistically, what are your chances of meeting Mr Right? Similarly, if your current relationship is sapping your lifeblood, it's going to be very difficult to believe in yourself enough to make a life-changing decision about your career, for instance. It's very easy to create a vicious circle of self-fulfilling belief that you're just not worth it.

Moving on is easier if you're footloose and fancy free but what happens when you've invested more than a couple of months or have children to consider?

FOR BETTER, FOR WORSE

We all get married with the very best intentions – to make it work no matter what. But, as hard as we try not to, it's very easy to get complacent and take our relationship for granted, assuming that everything's OK and that your relationship will stand the test of time. But will it? It's so easy to get caught up in the trap of life, not stopping for a moment to consider whether your relationship's keeping up with you. After all, it'll always be there, right?

See for yourself. Take a moment to answer the questions below and really think hard before you answer. *Note: if you're hesitant in any way about any of your answers, tick No.*

Question	Yes	No
1 Are you able to talk to your partner about anything?	☐	☐
2 Do you know where you stand?	☐	☐
3 Have you discussed plans for the future?	☐	☐
4 Do you like his friends?	☐	☐
5 Does he support you when you're stressed at work?	☐	☐
6 Do you still have the same hopes and dreams?	☐	☐
7 Does he make you laugh even when you're blue?	☐	☐
8 Are you still attracted to him?	☐	☐
9 Do you know how he feels about you now?	☐	☐
10 Are you in love with him?	☐	☐
11 Will he be there for you no matter what?	☐	☐

Count up your No's and read your scores below

0–2 Not bad, I think you're in a good place, but perhaps you need to cultivate your communication skills to keep the passion alive. Be spontaneous, take each other out on a surprise date once a month and make a point of only discussing each other – not work, the children, the mortgage – just the two of you.

3–6 You're in a comfort zone, but it's never going to be a big fluffy duvet. Your relationship isn't so bad you want out, but you're constantly moaning to your friends about him. Get a grip, work on it. If you don't like the way it looks now, it isn't going to get a refurb any time soon, unless you do something about it. Come on, why settle for mediocre when you can have it all? What your relationship needs is some TLC. Instead of moaning about it, how about investing some time and energy into getting your relationship back on track? Look at the questions you answered 'No' to and think about what you can do to make them right. The sooner you act, the better chance you have of making it to the finish line with a smile on your face.

7–10 Your relationship leaves much to be desired. You need to assess what you're getting out of it. Is it simply that you want your children to have a stable home, or the fact that you just can't face the idea of moving on? Being in the dark about your future is not a constructive way to follow your dream – which he probably thinks is a load of hogwash anyway. Come on, girlfriend, you can do so much better than this. You only live once and change – however painful – might benefit everyone in the long run. Take the high road and find someone else who really pushes your buttons – in more ways than one. This might sound harsh, but when you decide to follow your dream you will be faced with some tough decisions if you really want to succeed, and you simply can't afford to take prisoners.

THE TEST OF TIME

Yes, it's true that all relationships go through their ups and downs. Yes, it's true that passion doesn't last for ever. Yes, it's true that relationships are hard work. But that doesn't mean they should drag you down.

Your partner is the one person that sees you in the raw, your true identity. No hiding behind glad rags or make-up. No pretences – just the way you are. It's unconditional love and acceptance (with certain boundaries, of course). I always tell my husband that I love him to death, but if he blows up like a balloon he's out of the door! Feel at home but don't get too comfortable. It's always good to keep each other on your toes: that way you don't lose sight of yourself and turn into a couch potato before you can blink. Even the best relationships need work to remain fresh and healthy, and there will always be times when that is easier than others.

But when your relationship becomes a place where you can no longer be yourself, where both the predictability and monotony of its existence converts you from a once bubbly, vivacious soul to a dispirited one lacking any desire for change, then my question for you is – who needs to change? You or him?

Ask yourself:

★ When did you last run down the stairs with excitement when your husband came home?

★ When did you last lie in bed and giggle?

★ When did you last reapply your lipstick before greeting him at the door?

★ When did you last wear a sexy nightie when you went to sleep?

★ When did you last wear a matching set of undies – just for the hell of it?

★ When did you last go away for a night of uninterrupted passion?

★ When did you last write him a love note?

★ Has your life become one of function not fun?

Can you see how easy it is to turn fun into function and vice versa? Come on, you're as young as you feel – which is probably around eighty if you can't even be bothered to skip down the stairs when your partner comes home.

KEEP THE FLAME ALIVE

Even the best relationships take work and require a little tender loving now and then – some more than others. It's particularly easy when you've been together for a long time to lose sight of each other. Make an effort to reconnect and spend even an occasional evening with just the two of you to remind yourselves of what you fell in love with in the first place.

Having children can significantly change the dynamics of a relationship, and your own childhood experiences of families might mean you have vastly different approaches to parenting. Sometimes the very things that first attracted you can become the most difficult to live with. The fun-loving independent nature of your partner can be less of a plus when he's still not back to help you at the end of a long day with a fretful toddler.

singles, spouses and significant others

Ten steps to put the spring back into your relationship

★ When the going gets tough, make an effort to reconnect and spend time together that's not just in front of the TV.

★ Even an occasional evening with just the two of you helps to remind you of the person you fell in love with.

★ Have fun – both quality romantic time alone and as a family.

★ Talk! Compare your hopes and dreams and discuss your plans for the future. The same basic personal values can often be expressed in different ways; it's only by talking that you'll discover if you still both want the same things.

★ Listen! He needs to be reminded that you're still his friend, not just his wife or the mother of his children.

★ Identify each other's needs.

★ Show your feelings – touch every day.

★ Argue positively. Having the freedom to disagree and show how you feel is healthy and helps to strengthen relationships.

★ Surprise him – take him out for dinner or treat him to a night in a hotel, even if it's only five minutes from home.

★ All relationships change over time and go through different stages. The question is, can you see the opportunities and hold on to the intimacy?

CHALLENGE YOUR RELATIONSHIP

For one week only (or longer if you're up for it), I want you to convert back to that person you were when you first met. I want you to do at least one thing you used to do when you were first together, every day.

Also, make a point of wearing something sexy (whatever your size) – and if you don't have anything, for goodness' sake go and treat yourself. And avoid anything beige or black – splash out on something a little more daring if you can. You'll be surprised at the difference it makes to the way you feel.

Most importantly, I want you to make sure that you are wearing lip gloss at all times during the day. In fact, I want you to cover your husband with lipstick kisses – wherever and whenever you see fit. This may drive him crazy, but who knows where it may lead.

And don't even try that 'I'm too tired' or 'the children need bathing' excuse. The reason you're always tired is because you've lost your zest for life. Get it back and you'll have double the energy you had before and a whole lot more fun.

POINT OF NO RETURN

If you take on the challenge and all you get is a shrug and a 'you're crazy' dismissal, it's time for a heart-to-heart. Between you and me that is – not him (yet). I want you to start identifying for yourself what you need from your relationship and what you're actually getting.

Once you're clear in your own mind, sit him down and talk through the things you'd like to change or problems that need addressing. It may seem obvious, but part of any worthwhile discussion is listening. If you have issues, it may well be that he does too and it's important you hear what he has to say. You may find the same things bother you both and agree on what needs to be done to make it work.

At the end, if he listens attentively and then makes a concerted effort to implement some of your suggestions as well as making positive suggestions of his own, then your relationship can only get better. If, on the other hand, you just get laughed at, you need to take a serious look at your life. Only you know the true realities of your situation, but you may have some difficult decisions to make.

singles, spouses and significant others

JUMPING SHIP

Before I continue, I just want to clarify that I'm not suggesting we all trade our relationships in for a more exciting prospect as soon as the going gets tough. Quite the contrary. I'm just asking you to think about your relationship and identify what's working for you and what's not, and to consider what you can do to make it stronger. One thing's for sure, to make fundamental changes to your life you need to have a solid foundation in place. If it's a little rocky, it's unlikely you'll make it across to the other side. What's more, it's sure as hell going to be a lot easier if your partner's on board, rather than clinging on to the edge of your imagination.

If you've taken on the challenge, have tried to reignite the passion but hit a brick wall, perhaps you need outside help from a relationship counsellor. Think of it as a relationship MOT – identifying what needs fixing is half the battle won.

Follow your heart and your instinct. Do what feels right and it will make you happy in the long run.

FRIEND OR FOE?

The same principles you apply to the relationship with your partner also apply to your friends. Just as you need to feel free to be yourself with your partner, you need to feel appreciated for who you are by your friends too.

This might seem like a completely ridiculous question, but how often do you de-clutter your friendship list? Sound a bit harsh? Answer this, do you spend time with people out of habit or because they energise you and really support you no matter what? Or do you spend time with them out of habit or duty, because you used to be great friends but now, if you're honest, you have less in common and seeing them tends to leave you feeling flat and deflated. Or perhaps the reason you still keep in touch with them is because you feel guilty if you don't.

When you're striving to be the best that you can be, not all your friends will champion you along the way. Some will be there for you when you're down, but not when you decide to change your reality into something sweeter and more rewarding. Others will support you through the changes, but won't still be there to celebrate your success.

This isn't necessarily a bad thing, as I truly believe people come into your life for a reason and when their job is done they naturally move on again. That said, those that don't naturally move on and start to envy your choices and eventual success will no longer energise you in the same way. In fact, spending time with them could chip away at your self-confidence, leaving you drained.

Friends are funny things. Some like it when you're down but don't want to know when you're up. Others only want to know you when you're on top and can't be bothered with anything less. I guess life's challenges will help you identify who those true friends really are. It certainly has for me.

CHANGING CIRCLES

Friendships change over time and, while some may grow closer, others gradually drift away. Just as female friends are intensely important when you are single, a close network of girlfriends going through the same experiences becomes vital for your sanity when you have children. Even though you may still be working, the support of other new mothers who know exactly what you're going through is irreplaceable. On the other hand, childfree friends might not understand why you don't feel like staying out late at a club any more.

When looking at your friendships, you should apply many of the same principles you applied when evaluating the relationship with your partner.

singles, spouses and significant others

Ask yourself:
★ Do you feel comfortable and relaxed with this person?
★ Do you have fun together and make one another laugh?
★ Can you tell her your problems and know they won't go any further?
★ Can you trust her to give you advice, which may not necessarily be what you want to hear, but which is in your best interests?
★ Does she confide and trust in you? (After all, friendship's a two-way thing.)
★ Would you turn to each other in a crisis?

'KEEP AWAY FROM THOSE WHO TRY TO BELITTLE YOUR AMBITIONS. SMALL PEOPLE ALWAYS DO THAT BUT THE REALLY GREAT MAKE YOU BELIEVE THAT YOU TOO CAN BECOME GREAT.' **MARK TWAIN**

My message to you is, don't be afraid to be selective when it comes to the people you spend your time with. You've got what it takes to be exceptional: don't waste your energy on people who see you as anything less than the truly fabulous creation you are. My mother always says you could count your true friends on one hand. The older I get, the more I believe this is true. It's not a popularity contest; it's about surrounding yourself with people who really care about you.

FAMILY MATTERS

No chapter on relationships would be complete without something on that thorny topic, family. Don't get me wrong, I love my own family dearly and we generally get on well – though we do live on different continents! But there is no doubt that a great deal of the emotional baggage that many people cart around with them can be traced back to the relationship they have with their family.

The first significant relationships you have in life are formed with members of your family. In particular, how your parents and siblings relate to you and each other is crucial in developing your understanding of relationships generally and how you see yourself. You tend to believe the labels you're given as a child – so if you were seen as the quiet, placid one while your sister was the fiery demanding type, you'll often carry on in that role as an adult, and certainly when you're with your family.

It's important to remember that you learn throughout your life. You don't have to carry on in the same role if it's no longer who you are. Like all relationships, those with your family shift over time and changes are always stressful.

Learning how to communicate – talking and listening to one another – is the first vital step in building better relations (no pun intended). This is the only way you will ever understand each other and make sure you are viewed as the successful, dynamic grown-up you've become.

And don't forget that your family knows you better than most. They've seen you at your best and worst and still love you. There are probably no more loyal supporters in your journey to change your life and live out your dreams.

A FRIEND FOR LIFE

I've said it before and I'll say it again. To be a true master of your destiny, it's crucial that you surround yourself with champions – people who totally believe in you 100 per cent. Anyone who doesn't isn't worthy of being part of your inner circle. Spend less time with them and more with those who really care. Positive relationships will inspire and excite you to forge ahead, rain or shine.

CHAPTER NINE

'The only real failure in life is the failure to try'

So here's the deal – there isn't one. No man, no hotshot career or wardrobe to die for, no silver lining, no magic wand, nor a miracle diet. All that there is, is you. The moment you stop reading this book, you're on your own.

You don't believe me? Imagine I'm going to drop you in the middle of nowhere and you have to find your way onwards to somewhere on your own. Panic? Yip, that's probably how it's going to feel. 'You're kidding?' you ask. Not really, but feel free to stay in denial as long as you need, it's not going to affect me.

My point is this: it's great to feel inspired, it's wonderful to feel passionate, it's downright marvellous to have dreams and ideas – but they're all empty promises, missed opportunities, dead, forgotten, never to be seen or heard of again if you never do anything about them.

Of course, not all our dreams will come true, but the longer you procrastinate, the more time you waste on meaningless tasks that we all call a routine, the less time you'll have to create and mould your true destiny. So what if you're not the smartest, hottest talent around? So what if you've got no experience or have never ever been slim. Who's to say that what you've become is what you're meant to be? Only you.

It really is time to stop blaming the world and take responsibility for your frustrations. To hell with them, find another way of doing and living and, before you know it, life itself will become a more enjoyable place to be.

'the only real failure in life is the failure to try'

I remember when I was studying for my honours in Dietetics. There was a girl in the class who always tried to put me down. From the moment I opened my mouth she'd start to criticise me. No matter how hard I tried, I wasn't good enough or smart enough. She was determined to make me feel insignificant and stupid in every way possible – and it worked. It used to eat me up inside. I'd moan about her to my parents, my friends; I was eternally in fear of her acerbic tongue and her critical eye.

Without me realising it, she was controlling my life.

Then one day I was ranting on about her – again – to a friend, who just sat and listened to all my expletives. At the end he said to me, 'Stop hitting the ball back.'

'What?' I looked at him confused.

'Stop playing her game,' he said.

'But I'm not playing her game – she's the one who's making my life a misery, it's not my fault she's such a bitch …' He was beginning to irritate me.

Eventually I got it (sometimes it takes a little longer for blondes like me). It *was* my fault! I was allowing her to break me down and knock my confidence – I was giving her a licence to control me, my life, and everything in it. No one's ever worth that much.

I needed to find a way to change the dynamic, believe in myself and take control of my own destiny. So I got smart. I worked harder so that every time she tried to catch me out, I had the answer. And it worked. At the end of the year I moved up from bottom to the top of the class and graduated with honours.

SEIZE THE MOMENT

If you really want to make your dreams a reality – which you obviously do otherwise you wouldn't be reading this book – stop blaming the world and start making things happen. Not tomorrow, not next week or even next year, but *right now*.

It doesn't have to be big. It could be as small as clearing out your closet or as major as resigning from your job. The key is to recognise the things that are dragging you down and sapping all the energy from your bones. It's not that you're too old or too tired, it's just that your life the way it is right now is unexciting and dull. The minute you do something different, whether it's simply changing the side of the bed you sleep on or the colour of your hair, you will have broken the tedium and opened up the gap for opportunity to come in once again.

I remember a particular time when I was feeling really despondent about life and the harsh reality of 'living the dream'. I was finding it very tough to keep believing and continue to push ahead when there were no signs that things we going to change or improve any time soon. Suzy sent me a quote, which I often refer to when I'm having doubts about myself and the way forward.

'COURAGE DOES NOT ALWAYS ROAR. SOMETIMES COURAGE IS THE SMALL, QUIET VOICE AT THE END OF THE DAY SAYING 'I WILL TRY AGAIN TOMORROW.''
MARY ANNE RADMACHER

LIFE MOVES ON – WILL YOU?

Thank goodness for a new day, a new week and a new year. Imagine if life was just a series of hours with no definite beginning or end. We'd never have the extra push of an ideal opportunity to start afresh, to make a new beginning.

Irrespective of how many fresh starts you've already had, no one's going to limit the number of times you begin again. Who's keeping tabs anyway?

'the only real failure in life is the failure to try'

Keep on going until you get it right. And when you do, I want to hear all about it, because it's going to be huge – I can feel it in my bones. You are going to be one of the select few who make it to the other side and have the opportunity to appreciate the reason for struggling through.

PIGEON OR DOVE?

I've said it before and I'll say it again. This is your opportunity to move on with your life and do something extraordinary. It's your opportunity to stand out from the crowd. How many times have you been to a drinks party or work function and marvelled at the fact that everyone looks the same. No one has anything interesting or novel to say. Somehow all the big ideas everyone had at twenty seem to have evaporated by forty.

It's a bit like a flock of pigeons – you can't tell one from the next; they live off the scraps life has to offer them and don't tend to venture beyond their reality.

Now imagine you are a dove that flies into that flock of pigeons. You will be the shining star in a sea of grey. Everyone will be interested to learn more about you and what you've done. You will then leave and continue on to pastures new, only to return ten years later and find that nothing has changed, and everyone looks the same, just a bit rounder and older than they did before. Pigeon or dove? You choose.

KEEP SMILING THROUGH

And you know why? Your sense of humour needs to become your best friend. It will get you through when your worst nightmare comes true.

'the only real failure in life is the failure to try'

Christmas 2001, I'd been running my styling business for almost six months and I was struggling to keep the clients coming through the door. Suzy suggested I do some marketing to tap into the pre-Christmas rush. So I designed and printed a leaflet entitled: 'Get Yourself a New Woman for Christmas'. My idea was to target City bankers in the hope that they would all buy gift vouchers for their wives for Christmas. Result, so I thought.

I decided to hire a couple of models for impact and they positioned themselves at the top of the main escalators at Canary Wharf tube station. We handed out all the leaflets and then it was just a matter of waiting for that phone to ring. Eventually it did, and you know what he wanted: A NEW WOMAN FOR CHRISTMAS – literally! I was mortified. I thought I was being so clever and all I got was a dodgy geezer calling me up and asking me what our hourly rates were.

It's at moments like these when it's simply too much effort to cry and laughing makes you feel a whole lot better – especially mixed with a good bottle of wine. The bad news was that I didn't make my fortune that Christmas; the good news was that I laughed and learned a lot.

Taking on any transformational project, whether it be your body or your career, is supposed to be fun. It's supposed to fill you with exhilaration and excitement at the challenges – and more importantly the rewards – that lie ahead. If you're going to walk around with a scowl all over your face then I can assure you it's going to be a long, painful process, not just for you but for everyone else around you.

'the only real failure in life is the failure to try'

Next time you start to feel the fear and your demons are doing their best to get their claws into your soul, sit back and smile. Sounds crazy, I know, but the simple act of smiling will help deflect those feelings of gloom and despair. Try it out for yourself and see.

Or if, like me, a new handbag or pair of shoes is guaranteed to put the biggest grin on your face – hey, splash out. In the days when money was tight, or rather nonexistent, I would go out and buy a new handbag and then return it a week later (unused of course). The simple fact of being able to purchase it (on credit) made me feel successful and put a smile on my face. And, after a week of looking at something day-in day-out, you're so over it anyway!

The same principle applies if you're determined to drop a dress size. In those moments of weakness, raid the high street instead of your fridge – within reason, of course, but you get my drift. Being able to identify the small things that will help you step out of the depths of despair and make you feel like you're in control again and life is good: those are the things that will ultimately define your success.

'KEEP YOUR DREAMS ALIVE. UNDERSTAND TO ACHIEVE ANYTHING REQUIRES FAITH AND BELIEF IN YOURSELF, VISION, HARD WORK, DETERMINATION, AND DEDICATION. REMEMBER ALL THINGS ARE POSSIBLE FOR THOSE WHO BELIEVE.' **GAIL DEVERS**

'the only real failure in life is the failure to try'

YESTERDAY, TODAY, TOMORROW

This, my friends, is the point where I set you free to embark on the journey that will change your life in whatever way you choose. By now you know a lot more about me. I hope there have been elements in this book that have made you smile, and others that have fired up your passion and determination. It's all very well sitting here telling you the how, the why, and the wherefore, but if all you're going to do is add *Top to Toe* to your bookshelf and never think about it again, then I have failed miserably.

My mission has been to encourage you to think outside the boundaries of your current existence and question the way you live and the decisions you make each and every day. You see, you are a product of your own making; you are not a victim of misfortune. You can either accept your life and the way you live and look, or you can do something about changing the outcome. Every road you take will lead you to a different destination. Where you end up is a mystery … but be sure to enjoy the ride!

'the only real failure in life is the failure to try'

ACKNOWLEDGEMENTS

This book is the product of hard work and dedication from a lot of people

Firstly, thanks to my agent Julian Alexander, who was the powerhouse behind this book and whose constant support and encouragement made it possible.

Secondly to the staff at Hodder, who have made me feel part of the family and my book the focus of their publishing universe. In particular, to Rowena for believing in me, Helen for supporting me all the way and Emma for ensuring the world at large knows about *Top to Toe*.

To Karen for keeping the book afloat when I was drowning under my ever increasing workload – your support was invaluable.

To everyone at Smith & Gilmour for their creative talents – the design of the book is truly sensational.

To Si Scott for his absolutely gorgeous illustrations.

To Liam Duke for making me look like a supermodel – well almost.

To Amy, Cornelius and Gayle for all the hard work they put in to transform me from Top to Toe.

Special thanks must also go to Suzy Greaves for her invaluable insight, Andrew Barton for his hair mastery and Ruby Hammer for her make-up master class.